Principles
in Practice

The Principles in Practice imprint offers teachers concrete illustrations of effective classroom practices based in NCTE research briefs and policy statements. Each book discusses the research on a specific topic, links the research to an NCTE brief or policy statement, and then demonstrates how those principles come alive in practice: by showcasing actual classroom practices that demonstrate the policies in action; by talking about research in practical, teacher-friendly language; and by offering teachers possibilities for rethinking their own practices in light of the ideas presented in the books. Books within the imprint are grouped in strands, each strand focused on a significant topic of interest.

Volumes in the Adolescent Literacy Strand

Adolescent Literacy at Risk? The Impact of Standards (2009) Rebecca Bowers Sipe

Adolescent Literacy at Risk?

The Impact of Standards

Rebecca Bowers Sipe
Eastern Michigan University

NCTE

National Council of Teachers of English
1111 W. Kenyon Road, Urbana, Illinois 61801-1096

Staff Editor: Carol Roehm-Stogsdill

Imprint Editor: Cathy Fleischer

Interior Design: Victoria Pohlmann

Cover Design: Pat Mayer

Cover Images: Jerry Thompson at Thompson-McClellan Photography

NCTE Stock Number: 22969

Library of Congress Cataloging-in-Publication Data

Sipe, Rebecca Bowers.
    Adolescent literacy at risk? : the impact of standards / Rebecca Bowers Sipe.
        p. cm.
    Includes biliographical references and index.
    ISBN 978-0-8141-2296-9 ((pbk))
    1. Reading (Secondary)—United States. 2. Reading comprehension—United States.
3. Language arts (Secondary)—United States. 4. Education—Standards—United
States. I. Title.
    LB1632.S53 2009
    428.4071'2—dc22
                                                                    2009012200

For all the teachers who struggle daily to provide quality literacy experiences for the diverse learners who come into their lives.

Contents

Acknowledgments

Books often represent a memoir of a quest—to solve a problem, unravel a dilemma, or achieve some new set of possibilities. Just as with most quests, mine could not have been possible without the collaboration and support of many remarkable individuals. Throughout my career, I've found myself surrounded by a community of educators who have helped me raise questions, explore answers, and experiment with ideas. It was with educators such as these that I first allowed myself to confront questions of educational equity in a school district and within a state that represented then—and now—an enormously diverse merging of languages, cultures, and ethnic groups. Today, because of educators who share the same passion for making the lives of young people better, I continue to have the support needed to confront issues of educational equity and the impact of standards and testing on it.

In truth, this book emerges from a career-long quest dedicated to investigating ways to make reading and writing more accessible, functional, and uplifting for all of the diverse students with whom I've been fortunate enough to work. Little did I suspect at the outset how the conversation would come to embrace a battle of metaphors that has extended to the present and that continues to place enormous questions before us: Will we move forward treating adolescents as identical, interchangeable parts in a factory-styled system of learning, or will we finally recognize that learners are unique, gifted in many different ways, and blessed with a host of abilities through which they can best demonstrate their learning? In short, will we abandon misplaced metaphors of the factory and replace them with ones that reflect the organic process that quality literacy education should represent? If we can do that, then the vision of standards as a possibility for elevating the conversations of teachers, supporting their planning for exciting and challenging lessons, may be realized. I hope this book will contribute to that ongoing and important conversation.

I am so grateful to the individuals and groups who have helped me ask questions that mattered to me. From years back in Alaska, I recall with fondness intense conversations with passionate teachers such as Barbara Bernard, Harry Matrone, Kathy Hawkins, all fellows in the Anchorage Writing Project, as well as a host of other individuals who challenged and inspired me. Upon my move to Michigan, I once again found myself immersed in a rich teacher research network through the

Eastern Michigan Writing Project (EMWP) that has allowed me to enter many classrooms so that I could watch high standards in action. I owe a special thanks to my university and my colleagues for the support and encouragement they provide, and particularly I thank my EMWP colleagues Bill Tucker, Doug Baker, John Staunton, and Cathy Fleischer.

The effect of educational standards in classrooms, schools, and school districts across the United States is enormous, and it is imperative that all involved in creating and implementing them—from policymakers and legislators to educators—understand who is benefiting from standards as currently conceived and who may be placed at even greater risk. I am deeply grateful to teachers in the Washtenaw, Jackson, and Oakland schools for opening their doors to me. I thank individuals such as Allen Webb, Ellen Brinkley, and Linda Adler-Kassner, who helped so much with the Michigan standards project, and individuals such as Laura Schiller, Sarah Andrew-Vaughan, and Kathryn Bell who have devoted so much effort to helping teachers translate standards into practice.

I owe a particular thank you to a person who has helped and inspired me for more than a decade. Cathy Fleischer is a valued colleague and a good friend. She's also a remarkable editor who has worked closely with me to bring this book into being. No one could ask for a better advocate. She and the supportive staff at NCTE are simply the best.

Adolescent Literacy
An NCTE Policy Research Brief

Causes for Concern

It is easy to summon the language of crisis in discussing adolescent literacy. After all, a recent study of writing instruction reveals that 40 percent of high school seniors never or rarely write a paper of three or more pages, and although 4th and 8th graders showed some improvement in writing between 1998 and 2002, the scores of 12th graders showed no significant change. Less than half of the 2005 ACT-tested high school graduates demonstrated readiness for college-level reading, and the 2005 National Assessment of Educational Progress (NAEP) reading scores for 12th graders showed a decrease from 80 percent at the *proficient* level in 1992 to 73 percent in 2005.

Recent NAEP results also reveal a persistent achievement gap between the reading and writing scores of whites and students of color in 8th and 12th grades. Furthermore, both whites and students of color scored lower in reading in 2005 as compared with 1992, and both male and female students also scored lower in 2005.[1]

The challenges associated with adolescent literacy extend beyond secondary school to both college and elementary school. Many elementary school teachers worry about the 4th-grade slump in reading abilities. Furthermore, preliminary analysis of reading instruction in the elementary school suggests that an emphasis on processes of how to read can crowd out attention to reading for ideas, information, and concepts—the very skills adolescents need to succeed in secondary school. In the other direction, college instructors claim that students arrive in their classes ill-prepared to take up the literacy tasks of higher education, and employers lament the inadequate literacy skills of young workers. In our increasingly "flat" world, the U.S. share of the global college-educated workforce has fallen from 30 percent to 14 percent in recent decades as young workers in developing nations demonstrate employer-satisfying proficiency in literacy.[2]

In this context, many individuals and groups, including elected officials, governmental entities, foundations, and media outlets—some with little knowledge of the field—have stepped forward to shape policies that impact literacy instruction. Notably, the U.S. Congress is currently discussing new Striving Readers legislation (Bills S958 and HR2289) designed to improve the literacy skills of middle and high school students. Test scores and other numbers do not convey the full complexity of literacy even though they are effective in eliciting a feeling of crisis. Accordingly, a useful alternative would be for teachers and other informed professionals to take an interest in policy that shapes literacy instruction. This document provides research-based information to support that interest.

Common Myths about Adolescent Literacy

Myth: Literacy refers only to reading.

Reality: Literacy encompasses reading, writing, and a variety of social and intellectual practices that call upon the voice as well as the eye and hand. It also extends to new media—including nondigitized multimedia, digitized multimedia, and hypertext or hypermedia.[3]

Adolescent Literacy

Myth: Students learn everything about reading and writing in elementary school.

Reality: Some people see the processes of learning to read and write as similar to learning to ride a bicycle, as a set of skills that do not need further development once they have been achieved. Actually literacy learning is an ongoing and nonhierarchical process. Unlike math where one principle builds on another, literacy learning is recursive and requires continuing development and practice.[4]

Myth: Literacy instruction is the responsibility of English teachers alone.

Reality: Each academic content area poses its own literacy challenges in terms of vocabulary, concepts, and topics. Accordingly, adolescents in secondary school classes need explicit instruction in the literacies of each discipline as well as the actual content of the course so that they can become successful readers and writers in all subject areas.[5]

Myth: Academics are all that matter in literacy learning.

Reality: Research shows that out-of-school literacies play a very important role in literacy learning, and teachers can draw on these skills to foster learning in school. Adolescents rely on literacy in their identity development, using reading and writing to define themselves as persons. The discourses of specific disciplines and social/cultural contexts created by school classrooms shape the literacy learning of adolescents, especially when these discourses are different and conflicting.[6]

Myth: Students who struggle with one literacy will have difficulty with all literacies.

Reality: Even casual observation shows that students who struggle with reading a physics text may be excellent readers of poetry; the student who has difficulty with word problems in math may be very comfortable with historical narratives. More important, many of the literacies of adolescents are largely invisible in the classroom. Research on reading and writing beyond the classroom shows that students often have literacy skills that are not made evident in the classroom unless teachers make special efforts to include them.[7]

Myth: School writing is essentially an assessment tool that enables students to show what they have learned.

Reality: While it is true that writing is often central to assessment of what students have learned in school, it is also a means by which students learn and develop. Research shows that informal writing to learn can help increase student learning of content material, and it can even improve the summative writing in which students show what they have learned.[8]

Understanding Adolescent Literacy

Overview: Dimensions of Adolescent Literacy

In adolescence, students simultaneously begin to develop important literacy resources and experience unique literacy challenges. By fourth grade many students have learned a number of the basic processes of reading and writing; however, they still need to master literacy practices unique to different levels, disciplines, texts, and situations. As adolescents experience the shift to content-area learning, they need help from teachers to develop the confidence and skills necessary for specialized academic literacies.

Adolescents also begin to develop new literacy resources and participate in multiple discourse communities in and out of school. Frequently students' extracurricular literacy proficiencies are not valued in school. Literacy's link to community and identity means that it can be a site of resistance for adolescents. When students are not recognized for bringing valuable, multiple-literacy practices to school, they can become resistant to school-based literacy.[9]

1. Shifting Literacy Demands

The move from elementary to secondary school entails many changes including fundamental ones in the nature of literacy requirements. For adolescents, school-based literacy shifts as students engage with disciplinary content and a wide variety of difficult texts and writing tasks. Elementary school usually prepares students in the processes of reading, but many adolescents do not understand the multiple dimensions of content-based literacies. Adolescents may struggle with reading in some areas and do quite well with others. They may also be challenged to write in ways that conform to new disciplinary discourses. The proliferation of high-stakes tests can complicate the literacy learning of adolescents, particularly if test preparation takes priority over content-specific literacy instruction across the disciplines.[10]

Research says . . .

- Adolescents are less likely to struggle when subject area teachers make the reading and writing approaches in a given content area clear and visible.
- Writing prompts in which students reflect on their current understandings, questions, and learning processes help to improve content-area learning.[11]
- Effective teachers model how they access specific content-area texts.
- Learning the literacies of a given discipline can help adolescents negotiate multiple, complex discourses and recognize that texts can mean different things in different contexts.
- Efficacious teaching of cross-disciplinary literacies has a social justice dimension as well as an intellectual one.[12]

2. Multiple and Social Literacies

Adolescent literacy is social, drawing from various discourse communities in and out of school. Adolescents already have access to many different discourses including those of ethnic, online, and popular culture communities. They regularly use literacies for social and political purposes as they create meanings and participate in shaping their immediate environments.[13]

Teachers often devalue, ignore, or censor adolescents' extracurricular literacies, assuming that these literacies are morally suspect, raise controversial issues, or distract adolescents

Adolescent Literacy

from more important work. This means that some adolescents' literacy abilities remain largely invisible in the classroom.[14]

Research says . . .

- The literacies adolescents bring to school are valuable resources, but they should not be reduced to stereotypical assumptions about predictable responses from specific populations of students.
- Adolescents are successful when they understand that texts are written in social settings and for social purposes.
- Adolescents need bridges between everyday literacy practices and classroom communities, including online, non-book-based communities.
- Effective teachers understand the importance of adolescents finding enjoyable texts and don't always try to shift students to "better" books.[15]

3. Importance of Motivation

Motivation can determine whether adolescents engage with or disengage from literacy learning. If they are not engaged, adolescents with strong literacy skills may choose not to read or write. The number of students who are not engaged with or motivated by school learning grows at every grade level, reaching epidemic proportions in high school. At the secondary level, students need to build confidence to meet new literacy challenges because confident readers are more likely to be engaged. Engagement is encouraged through meaningful connections.[16]

Research says . . .

Engaged adolescents demonstrate internal motivation, self-efficacy, and a desire for mastery. Providing student choice and responsive classroom environments with connections to "real life" experiences helps adolescents build confidence and stay engaged.[17]

A. Student Choice

- Self-selection and variety engage students by enabling ownership in literacy activities.
- In adolescence, book selection options increase dramatically, and successful readers need to learn to choose texts they enjoy. If they can't identify pleasurable books, adolescents often lose interest in reading.
- Allowing student choice in writing tasks and genres can improve motivation. At the same time, writing choice must be balanced with a recognition that adolescents also need to learn the literacy practices that will support academic success.
- Choice should be meaningful. Reading materials should be appropriate and should speak to adolescents' diverse interests and varying abilities.
- Student-chosen tasks must be supported with appropriate instructional support or scaffolding.[18]

B. Responsive Classroom Environments

- Caring, responsive classroom environments enable students to take ownership of literacy activities and can counteract negative emotions that lead to lack of motivation.

- Instruction should center around learners. Active, inquiry-based activities engage reluctant academic readers and writers. Inquiry-based writing connects writing practices with real-world experiences and tasks.
- Experiences with task-mastery enable increased self-efficacy, which leads to continued engagement.
- Demystifying academic literacy helps adolescents stay engaged.
- Using technology is one way to provide learner-centered, relevant activities. For example, many students who use computers to write show more engagement and motivation and produce longer and better papers.
- Sustained experiences with diverse texts in a variety of genres that offer multiple perspectives on life experiences can enhance motivation, particularly if texts include electronic and visual media.[19]

4. Value of Multicultural Perspectives

Monocultural approaches to teaching can cause or increase the achievement gap and adolescents' disengagement with literacy. Students should see value in their own cultures and the cultures of others in their classrooms. Students who do not find representations of their own cultures in texts are likely to lose interest in school-based literacies. Similarly, they should see their home languages as having value. Those whose home language is devalued in the classroom will usually find school less engaging.

Research says . . .

Multicultural literacy is seeing, thinking, reading, writing, listening, and discussing in ways that critically confront and bridge social, cultural, and personal differences. It goes beyond a "tourist" view of cultures and encourages engagement with cultural issues in all literature, in all classrooms, and in the world.[20]

A. Multicultural Literacy across All Classrooms

- Multicultural education does not by itself foster cultural inclusiveness because it can sometimes reinforce stereotypical perceptions that need to be addressed critically.
- Multicultural literacy is not just a way of reading "ethnic" texts or discussing issues of "diversity," but rather is a holistic way of *being* that fosters social responsibility and extends well beyond English/language arts classrooms.
- Teachers need to acknowledge that we all have cultural frameworks within which we operate, and everyone—teachers and students alike—needs to consider how these frameworks can be challenged or changed to benefit all peoples.[21]
- Teacher knowledge of social science, pedagogical, and subject-matter content knowledge about diversity will foster adolescents' learning.
- Successful literacy development among English language learners depends on and fosters collaborative multicultural relationships among researchers, teachers, parents, and students.
- Integration of technology will enhance multicultural literacy.

- Confronting issues of race and ethnicity within classrooms and in the larger community will enhance student learning and engagement.[22]

B. Goals of Multicultural Literacy

- Students will view knowledge from diverse ethnic and cultural perspectives, and use knowledge to guide action that will create a humane and just world.
- Teachers will help students understand the whiteness studies principle that white is a race so they can develop a critical perspective on racial thinking by people of all skin colors.
- Multicultural literacy will serve as a means to move between cultures and communities and develop transnational understandings and collaboration.
- Ideally, students will master basic literacies *and* become mulitculturally literate citizens who foster a democratic multicultural society.[23]

Research-Based Recommendations for Effective Adolescent Literacy Instruction

For teachers . . .

Research on the practices of highly effective adolescent literacy teachers reveals a number of common qualities. Teachers who have received recognition for their classroom work, who are typically identified as outstanding by their peers and supervisors, and whose students consistently do well on high-stakes tests share a number of qualities. These qualities, in order of importance, include the following:

1. teaching with approaches that foster critical thinking, questioning, student decision-making, and independent learning;
2. addressing the diverse needs of adolescents whose literacy abilities vary considerably;
3. possessing personal characteristics such as caring about students, being creative and collaborative, and loving to read and write;
4. developing a solid knowledge about and commitment to literacy instruction;
5. using significant quality and quantity of literacy activities including hands-on, scaffolding, mini-lessons, discussions, group work, student choice, ample feedback, and multiple forms of expression;
6. participating in ongoing professional development;
7. developing quality relationships with students; and
8. managing the classroom effectively.[24]

For school programs . . .

Research on successful school programs for adolescent literacy reveals fifteen features that contribute to student achievement:

1. direct and explicit instruction;
2. effective instructional principles embedded in content;

3. motivation and self-directed learning;

4. text-based collaborative learning;

5. strategic tutoring;

6. diverse texts;

7. intensive writing;

8. technology;

9. ongoing formative assessment of students;

10. extended time for literacy;

11. long-term and continuous professional development, especially that provided by literacy coaches;

12. ongoing summative assessment of students and programs;

13. interdisciplinary teacher teams;

14. informed administrative and teacher leadership; and

15. comprehensive and coordinated literacy program.[25]

For policymakers . . .

A national survey produced action steps for policymakers interested in fostering adolescent literacy. These include:

1. align the high school curriculum with postsecondary expectations so that students are well prepared for college;

2. focus state standards on the essentials for college and work readiness;

3. shape high school courses to conform with state standards;

4. establish core course requirements for high school graduation;

5. emphasize higher-level reading skills across the high school curriculum;

6. make sure students attain the skills necessary for effective writing;

7. ensure that students learn science process and inquiry skills; and

8. monitor and share information about student progress.[26]

This report is produced by NCTE's James R. Squire Office of Policy Research, directed by Anne Ruggles Gere, with assistance from Laura Aull, Hannah Dickinson, Melinda McBee Orzulak, and Ebony Elizabeth Thomas, all students in the Joint PhD Program in English and Education at the University of Michigan.

Notes

1. ACT. (2006). *Aligning postsecondary expectations and high school practice: The gap defined: Policy implications of the ACT national curriculum survey results 2005–2006.* Iowa City, IA. Retrieved on July 3, 2007, from http://www.act.org/path/policy/pdf/NationalCurriculum Survey2006.pdf

Adolescent Literacy

Applebee, A., & Langer, J. (2006). *The state of writing instruction in America's schools: What existing data tell us*. Center on English Learning and Achievement. Retrieved on July 3, 2007, from http://cela.albany.edu

National Center for Education Statistics. (2002). *National Assessment of Educational Progress (NAEP). NAEP Writing–Average writing scale score results, grades 4, 8, and 12: 1998 and 2002*. Retrieved on July 3, 2007, from http://nces.ed.gov/nationsreportcard/writing/results2002/natscalescore.asp

National Center for Education Statistics. (2006). *National Assessment of Educational Progress (NAEP). Reading Results: Executive Summary for Grades 4 and 8*. Retrieved on July 3, 2007, from http://nces.ed.gov/nationsreportcard/reading/

2. Altwerger, B., Arya, P., Jin, L., Jordan, N. L., et al. (2004). When research and mandates collide: The challenges and dilemmas of teacher education in the era of NCLB. *English Education, 36*, 119–133.

National Center on Education and the Economy. (2007). *Tough choices or tough times: The report of the New Commission on the Skills of the American Workforce*. San Francisco, CA: Jossey-Bass.

3. Brandt, D. (2001). *Literacy in American lives*. New York: Cambridge University Press.

Gee, J. (2007). *Social linguistics and literacies: Ideology in discourses*. London: Taylor & Francis.

4. Franzak, J. K. (2006). *Zoom*. A review of the literature on marginalized adolescent readers, literacy theory, and policy implications. *Review of Educational Research, 76, 2*, 209–248.

5. Sturtevant, E., & Linek, W. (2003). The instructional beliefs and decisions of middle and secondary teachers who successfully blend literacy and content. *Reading Research & Instruction, 43*, 74–90.

6. Guzzetti, B., & Gamboa, M. (2004). 'Zines for social justice: Adolescent girls writing on their own. *Reading Research Quarterly, 39*, 408–437.

Langer, J. (2001). Beating the odds: Teaching middle and high school students to read and write well. *American Educational Research Journal, 38, 4*, 837–880.

Nielsen, L. (2006). Playing for real: Texts and the performance of identity. In D. Alvermann, K. Hinchman, D. Moore, S. Phelps, & D. Waff (Eds.), *Reconceptualizing the literacies in adolescents' lives* (2nd ed.) Mahwah, NJ: Lawrence Erlbaum, 5–28.

Sturtevant, E. & Linek, W. (2003).

7. Moje, E. B. (2002). Re-framing adolescent literacy research for new times: Studying youth as a resource. *Reading Research and Instruction, 41*, 211–228.

8. Boscolo, P., & Mason, L. (2001). Writing to learn, writing to transfer. In G. Jijlaarsdam, P. Tynjala, L. Mason, & K. Londa (Eds.), *Studies in writing: Vol 7. Writing as a learning tool: Integrating theory and practice*. Dordrecht, The Netherlands: Kluwer Academic Publishers, 83–104.

9. Lenters, K. (2006). Resistance, struggle, and the adolescent reader. *Journal of Adolescent and Adult Literacy, 50*(2), 136–142.

10. Moje, E. B., & Sutherland, L. M. (2003). The future of middle school literacy education. *English Education, 35*(2), 149–164.

Snow, C. E., & Biancarosa, G. (2003). *Adolescent literacy and the achievement: What do we know and where do we go from here?* New York: Carnegie Corporation. Retrieved June 23, 2007, from http://www.all4ed.org/resources/CarnegieAdolescentLiteracyReport.pdf

11. Bangert-Drowns, R. L., Hurley, M. M., & Wilkinson, B. (2004). The effects of school-based writing-to-learn interventions on academic achievement: A meta-analysis. *Review of Educational Research, 74*, 29–58.

Greenleaf, C. L., Schoenbach, R., Cziko, C., & Mueller, F. (2001). Apprenticing adolescent readers to academic literacy. *Harvard Education Review, 71*(1), 79–129.

12. Moje, E. B., Ciechanowski, K. M, Kramer, K., Ellis, L., Carrillo, R., & Collazo, T. (2004). Working toward third space in content area literacy: An examination of everyday funds of knowledge and discourse. *Reading Research Quarterly, 39*(1), 38–70.

13. Moje, E. B. (2007). Developing socially just subject-matter instruction: A review of the literature on disciplinary literacy. N. L. Parker (Ed.), *Review of research in education.* (pp. 1–44). Washington, DC: American Educational Research Association.

14. Kim, J. L. W., & Monique, L. (2004). Pleasure reading: Associations between young women's sexual attitudes and their reading of contemporary women's magazines. *Psychology of Women Quarterly, 28*(1), 48–58.

Kliewer, C., Biklen, D., & Kasa-Hendrickson, C. (2006). Who may be literate? Disability and resistance to the cultural denial of competence. *American Educational Research Journal, 43*(2), 163–192.

Moje, E. B., & Sutherland, L. M. (2003).

15. Moje, E. B. (2007).

Ross, C. S. (2001). Making choices: What readers say about choosing books for pleasure. In W. Katz (Ed.), *Reading, Books, and Librarians.* New York: Haworth Information Press.

16. Guthrie, J. T., Van Meter, P., McCann, A. D., Wigfield, A., Bennett, L., & Poundstone, C. C. (1996). Growth of literacy engagement: Changes in motivations and strategies during concept-oriented reading instruction. *Reading Research Quarterly, 31*, 306–332.

17. Guthrie, J. T. (2001). Contexts for engagement and motivation in reading. *Reading Online.* International Reading Association. Retrieved June 23, 2007, from http://www.readingonline.org/articles/handbook/guthrie/index.html

Guthrie, J. T., & Humenick, N. M. (2004). Motivating students to read: Evidence for classroom practices that increase reading motivation and achievement. In P. McCardle and V. Chhabra (Eds.), *The voice of evidence in reading research.* Baltimore, MD: Brookes, 329–54.

Adolescent Literacy

18. Biancarosa, G., & Snow, C. (2004). *Reading next: A vision for action and research in middle and high school literacy. Report to Carnegie Corporation of New York*. Washington, DC: Alliance for Excellent Education. Retrieved June 25, 2007, from http://www.all4ed.org/publications/ReadingNext/ReadingNext.pdf

Guthrie, J. T. (2001).

Oldfather, P. (1994). *When students do not feel motivated for literacy learning: How a responsive classroom culture helps*. College Park, MD: University of Maryland, National Reading Research Center. Retrieved June 25, 2007, from http://curry.edschool.virginia.edu/go/clic/nrrc/rspon_r8.html; NCREL (2005).

19. Goldberg, A., Russell, M., & Cook, A. (2003).The effects of computers on student writing: A meta-analysis of studies from 1992 to 2002. *Journal of Technology, Learning, and Assessment*, *2*, 1–51.

Greenleaf et al. (2001).

Guthrie, J. T. (2001).

Kamil, M. (2003).

Ray, K. W. (2006). Exploring inquiry as a teaching stance in the writing workshop. *Language Arts*, *83*(3), 238–248.

20. Hade, D. (1997). Reading multiculturally. In V. Harris (Ed.), *Using multiethnic literature in the K-8 classroom*. Norwood: Christopher-Gordon.

Cai, M. (1998). Multiple definitions of multicultural literature: Is the debate really just "ivory tower" bickering? *New Advocate*, *11*, 4, 11–24.

Taxel, J. (1992). The politics of children's literature: Reflections on multiculturalism, political correctness, and Christopher Columbus. In V. Harris (Ed.), *Teaching multicultural literature in grades K-8*. Norwood: Christopher-Gordon.

21. Fang, Z., Fu, D., & Lamme, L. (1999). Rethinking the role of multicultural literature in literacy instruction: Problems, paradox, and possibilities. *New Advocate*, *12*(3), 259–276.

Nieto, S. (2000). *Affirming diversity: The sociopolitical context of multicultural education*. New York: Longman.

Rochman, H. (1993). Beyond political correctness. In D. Fox & K. Short (Eds.), *Stories matter: The complexity of cultural authenticity in children's literature*. Urbana: NCTE.

Taxel, J. (1992).

22. Banks, J. A. (1991). Teaching multicultural literacy to teachers. *Teaching Education*, *4*, 1, 135–144.

Feuerverger, G. (1994). A multicultural literacy intervention for minority language students. *Language and Education*, *8*, 3, 123–146.

Diamond, B. J., & Moore, M. A. (1995). Multicultural literacy: Mirroring the reality of the classroom. New York: Longman.

Freedman, S. W. (1999). *Inside city schools: Investigating literacy in multicultural classrooms*. New York: Teachers College Press.

23. Banks, J. A. (2004). *Handbook of research on multicultural education*. San Francisco: Jossey-Bass.

Jay, G. S. (2005). Whiteness studies and the multicultural literature classroom. *MELUS, 30*(2), 99-121.

Luke, A., & Carpenter, M. (2003). Literacy education for a new ethics of global community. *Language Arts, 81*(1), 20.

24. Applebee, A., Langer, J., Nystrand, M., & Gamoran, A. (2003). Discussion-based approaches to developing understanding: Classroom instruction and student performance in middle and high school English. *American Educational Research Journal, 40*, 685–730.

Paris, S. R., & Block, C. C. (2007). The expertise of adolescent literacy teachers. *Journal of Adolescent & Adult Literacy, 50*, 7, 582–596.

25. Biancarosa, G., & Snow C. E. (2004).

26. ACT, 2006.

This publication of the James R. Squire Office of Policy Research offers updates on research with implications for policy decisions that affect teaching and learning. Each issue addresses a different topic. Download this issue at http://www.ncte.org/library/NCTEFiles/Resources/Positions/chron0907ResearchBrief.pdf.

1 Literacy at Risk?

Adolescent literacy concerns all of us. Because we are teachers who work closely with teen readers and writers, we know how important it is that students leave high school with adequate abilities to read, write, speak, listen, and work with media. We know that students who don't have these abilities are far less prepared to enter into the critical work of adult citizenry.

Our job as literacy teachers for adolescents, however, is complicated—even more so in recent years—by many factors, two of which I want to speak to in this book. The first is that not everyone agrees on the definition of literacy. Whether we are teachers, curriculum directors, administrators, parents, researchers, or policymakers, we do share a common concern for the development of strong literacy skills. What we may not agree on, though, is a fundamental definition of literacy: Exactly what is literacy today in a rapidly changing global society? More precisely, what types of knowledge, skills, strategies, and habits does a literate person need to possess in order to be productive, successful, and fully engaged in the world that is coming to be? This struggle to define what all students need to know and be able to do is not a new one, but it is one of unequaled importance right now.

Fortunately, as teachers, we know quite a bit about adolescent literacy (much of which is outlined in the Adolescent Literacy Brief included in this volume). We know, for example, that the demands of literacy shift dramatically for teens as they move from elementary to secondary schools with the requirements of disciplinary-based reading and writing. We know that as teens move among the multiple discourses of their many social encounters, they enact complex and varied forms of literacy, so much so that many of us now speak of *literacies* rather than literacy. We know that motivation is a key component in the literacies of our teens—and that many adolescents who were strong readers and writers in the elementary years become almost "aliterate" during those teen years. And we know that engagement is closely tied to full literacy—especially important as we consider multicultural perspectives.

The second complicating factor in our job as literacy teachers relates to this expanded notion of literacy: how does what we know about adolescent literacy fit into the parallel conversation that has captured the public's imagination—that of standards? Standards implementation efforts at the state and local levels, I argue in this book, may be the single most significant factor in supporting or derailing adolescent literacy initiatives across the nation. The vision that shapes standards at the state level and the ways those standards are perceived, implemented, and tested by local school districts play an enormous role in determining whether teachers have time, resources, and even energy for planning and delivering rich instruction that truly does represent world-class expectations. If the standards that are being imposed by states result in prescriptive and restrictive approaches that limit the ability of teachers to draw on their own expertise to meet the needs of adolescents, without a doubt adolescent learners will suffer.

As I've moved around the country talking with secondary teachers who struggle to address seemingly ever-increasing standards in English language arts, the vision of a funnel has solidified in my mind. At the narrow end of the funnel is the local classroom filled with restless adolescents. By all appearances, the classroom looks more similar than not to the one I attended in high school decades ago. Desks, books, a scattering of technology, and a solitary teacher define the learning space for an hour or more each day. Within that space and those precious moments of often interrupted instructional time, the teacher weaves a curriculum that addresses many of the most fundamental skills young people will need when they enter the world beyond the secondary school walls. Whether they go on to college—as many will—or directly into the workplace, being able to read and listen critically, to write and speak clearly and articulately, and to judiciously take in information from a host of media are essential skills for life in the twenty-first century.

However, though the contemporary classroom may look familiar, much has changed that influences instruction on a daily basis. Over the past three decades, endless reports, commission findings, and media coverage have produced a confused mix of policies, standards, and legislative acts. Though at first blush it might seem to be the case, the current "standards" that drive instructional decision making in public schools do *not* represent a single set of expectations. Instead, these expectations, coming from a host of sources—each representing a different perspective, set of biases, and political agenda—have been poured indiscriminately into the open funnel; too often these have descended upon the local classroom in a cacophony of expectations. By the time these competing demands are placed upon the local teacher, they are apt to conflate to a single implementation under the generic guise of "the standards." And too often these standards are imposed on the classroom along with tests, pacing guides, and other tools that both regulate and restrict the abilities of teachers to meet individual student needs or to draw upon their own unique areas of expertise.

Though it's true that each state has its own set of state-developed standards—some with far more specificity than others—each set still represents an amalgam of expectations influenced or mandated by a variety of groups. From private business-oriented organizations such as Achieve, Inc., to nonprofit and enormously powerful testing agents such as the College Board and ACT, many voices have added their expectations to the open end of the funnel, resulting in a proliferation of expectations targeting the classroom as developers of standards attempt to address a catalog of viewpoints and perspectives. As the new expectations represented by standards have become institutionalized in schools across the country, educators have often struggled to make sense of them. What are the purposes for these standards and expectations? What intentions frame their development? How can educators claim a role in shaping their development and implementation?

It's not just individual teachers who have felt weighted down by the burden of excessive and conflicting standards and expectations. High schools themselves have been under sharp scrutiny for more than two decades now, as publication after publication reminds a confused public of the failures of secondary schools, and questions about whether those failings are real or not are too often brushed aside in a wash of well-honed rhetoric. With the celebration of the twenty-fifth anniversary of *A Nation at Risk*, we have once again been bombarded with questions about how little progress has been made during the intervening years. In *Rising to the Challenge: Are High School Graduates Prepared for College and Work?*, a study conducted by Peter D. Hart Research Associates for Achieve, Inc., we heard yet again how unprepared high school graduates are in literacy and mathematics for the university or workplace. This report reminded readers that "[a]lthough public schools are doing a good job preparing many graduates, they are seriously failing a substantial minority" (2). Using the same alarmist rhetoric that stunned Americans in 1983 in *A Nation at Risk*, this document simultaneously reiterates the problems schools continue to face while also directing attention away from the fact that the *majority* of students are leaving schools well prepared for work and for college. Such global statements leave schools and teachers in a vulnerable position as they are forced to invest energy reacting to negative media and resisting quick-fix solutions to problems that may not even exist in their schools. This is due in large part to reform efforts that have tended to ignore both the expertise of practitioners and the contexts of particular schools.

In the thirty-five years I have worked in public education as a teacher, curriculum coordinator, school board member, and university professor, I have had remarkable experiences with outstanding English language arts educators from one end of the country to the other. Consistently, I have found teachers who know and care about their students, and who lose sleep working to craft lessons that will build the knowledge and skills students need to be successful in the world. These teachers, by and large, have been working to address adolescent literacy needs for years, striving diligently to create classrooms that reflect the highest standards possible.

Secondary teachers are experts in their fields. They are with students every day. Given time and support, they are fully capable of contributing creative solutions to complex problems. They cannot do so, however, without the resources—time, opportunity, and support—needed to do things differently; nor can they do so in isolation. For the conversations about school and curricular reform to be fruitful, their voices must be heard and the causes and solutions to current dilemmas regarding adolescent literacy must be situated within the context of the local community and society at large.

Literacy is *everybody's* business. We must be willing as a society to think hard about what all students need to know and be able to do within the context of English language arts. This consideration cannot lead merely to a compendium of information that catalogs all that is possible for an expert in literature or rhetoric to know. We must, instead, think carefully about the special role of reading, writing, speaking, listening, and viewing in the lives of all citizens, not just future English teachers.

This book represents my effort to understand the impact of the standards movement on adolescent literacy. Part 1 of this book examines the standards phenomena in order to begin a discussion of the impact of standards on local classrooms. In this discussion I try to unpack various representative standards and discuss the nature of the groups responsible for them. Throughout this discussion, I take readers back repeatedly to questions that frame the impact of various standards on local classrooms. By laying this foundation first, I hope to provide a context within which to examine the various reactions to standards and implementations of standards within classrooms of accomplished teachers presented in Part 2. Finally, in Part 3, I encourage readers to draw upon information from Part 1 and representations of research-based practice in Part 2 as they consider their own plans for improving adolescent literacy through local decision making.

We cannot succeed as a nation without a highly literate population. The next steps we take to promote adolescent literacy are critical ones. Drawing upon the recommendations described in *Adolescent Literacy: An NCTE Policy Research Brief* and using these as a frame, we can begin to move forward with literacy standards implementation in a thoughtful manner.

Chapter One

Entering the Conversation: Standards vs. Standardization

Our Nation is at risk. Our once unchallenged preeminence in commerce, industry, science, and technological innovation is being overtaken by competitors throughout the world. This report is concerned with only one of the many causes and dimensions of the problem, but it is the one that undergirds American prosperity, security, and civility. We report to the American people that while we can take justifiable pride in what our schools and colleges have historically accomplished and contributed to the United States and the well-being of its people, the educational foundations of our society are presently being eroded by a rising tide of mediocrity that threatens our very future as a Nation and a people. What was unimaginable a generation ago has begun to occur—others are matching and surpassing our educational attainments.

If an unfriendly foreign power had attempted to impose on America the mediocre educational performance that exists today, we might well have viewed it as an act of war. As it stands, we have allowed this to happen to ourselves. We have even squandered the gains in student achievement made in the wake of the Sputnik challenge. Moreover, we have dismantled essential support systems which helped make those gains possible. We have, in effect, been committing an act of unthinking, unilateral educational disarmament. (A Nation at Risk, 1983)

When I read *A Nation at Risk* in 1983, my career as a teacher, administrator, and future English educator was anchored in rich soil. My work was situated in a remarkably diverse school district that allowed me the opportunity to work with teachers drawn from all over the United States and Canada. In the flush of oil wealth that flowed into local school districts in Alaska in the early 1980s, my colleagues and I finally had resources that allowed us to pursue our dream of equitable literacy engagement for all of our students. Literacy leaders from across the country, lured by the promise of working in such a site, came north to help us explore and shape our visions for new and engaging literacy curricula. Those were days filled with promise and excitement, yet in the midst of that challenging work lurked the shadow of questions that continuously troubled us.

We found ourselves wrestling with very fundamental literacy concerns, many of which dealt with issues of equity. What constituted a quality literacy education for all of our adolescents? Whose literary traditions, which visions of literacy, and what types of demonstrations of literacy skill and knowledge should we privilege? What was it, after all, that all students needed to know and be able to do to achieve success when they moved from school into the world beyond our care? Moreover, how should we actually define literacy success amid the rampant technological and social change of the times?

As my fellow teachers and I pondered current research and learning theory within the context of our school district in Anchorage, we found ourselves reflecting upon the many inequities we observed. Even at that time our district was large. With nearly 40,000 students spanning a geographic area the size of the state of Delaware, we worked daily with individuals representing nearly one hundred different languages and very diverse learning needs. As we looked within and across our schools, we realized that our questions about equity were more complex than we had previously imagined.

Even within our single, albeit large, district, students in some schools seemed better prepared, their classrooms more equipped, their teachers more receptive to varied pedagogies and technologies. Even within our own schools—and sometimes within our own teaching—some of our secondary students were immersed in stimulating and challenging English classes, whereas others seemed to be mired in a stifling routine of learning "the basics": decoding texts, memorizing parts of speech, and literal recall of informational and literary facts within a tightly prescribed curriculum. Tracking of students appeared to encourage certain types of practices. Certainly the expectations framing the education of some adolescents were far from high, and those expectations were definitely not equal. In other cases, even when the curriculum and books provided were the same, student engagement and outcomes clearly were not.

I recall a particular occasion that helped us to frame our thinking and push our questions forward. As we sorted through our observations about our classrooms, we turned our reflections to our own educational histories. I found myself describing my first reunion with a diverse group of high school friends. As I did so, I was forced to consider—for the first time—the utter lack of equity and high standards characterizing the high school experiences of many of my classmates. My own classes were filled with college-bound students. Identified early—in many cases as early as the primary grades—we had moved through our local school system together. My recollections of school were laced with memories of spirited and practiced teachers like Mr. Hatley, who challenged us to consider the perspectives, special interests, and politics veiled in historical and current events. This amazing teacher opened history for us with a continuous string of deeply textured and nuanced stories. There also were new teachers such as Miss Jones who sauntered into class in tenth grade and innocently announced that we would not only read short stories but also write a book of short stories ourselves, hold a literary reading at which we would sell the books, and then have a party with the proceeds; and there was Mr. Whittington, a first-year teacher who was nearly fired for introducing our senior English class to culturally and politically charged literature before our rural southern community was ready. In each case these teachers not only opened for us engaging, challenging, and authentic work, but they also skillfully scaffolded the requisite strategies and skills we needed to be successful. Somehow along the way, however, I had failed to notice that students in other classes were not always offered the curriculum or methods that I enjoyed.

As I described my observations to my Alaskan teaching colleagues, I once again confronted the inequities that emerge when high expectations are not universally embraced. Had I not been among that class of college-bound students, how would my future have been different? Would I even have felt that a college education was within my grasp? As a student whose parents had not gone to college, who came from a family of meager means, it was hard to deny the impact of high expectations provided by my teachers on the subsequent academic choices and opportunities afforded me.

Interestingly, even as our teacher research group pondered questions about the English language arts programs in our schools, our school district was reporting excellent progress on most recognized literacy indicators. Steady score increases on required standardized tests, increasing high school graduation rates, and higher percentages of students moving through Advanced Placement classes and on to colleges around the nation all suggested that we were doing things right. Of note, these indicators of success from our district proved to be consistent with those reported nationally that suggested steady increases in each category (Stedman and Kaestle, 19–20). Moreover, as later reported by Myers, "by the 1980s, most states were reporting above-average results on norm-referenced tests of decoding literacy in reading" (107). And yet, despite all these reported gains, our teacher study group sensed that many of our students needed more.

Our process of thinking and reflecting together as teachers, of constantly turning the soil as we moved deeper and deeper into our questions, was one of my first experiences with teacher research. As we questioned, reflected, investigated, and made observations, we found ourselves with even more—and often more troubling—questions, leading to more research. Our district provided equal funding for all of its schools, equivalent funding for materials, and equal pay for teachers. And yet we could all describe a host of inequities that we observed—most often in schools that provided services to our most disadvantaged students. Our initial inquiries were founded on our desire to create challenging experiences through literacy-rich classrooms for all of our students. Now, we began to question whether even careful attention to equity of resources would be sufficient to ensure a level playing field for all.

In 1983 the opening paragraphs of *A Nation at Risk* ignited a concern for me that has underscored much of my professional work since. Despite the alarmist tone of the document and its simplistic solutions to complicated problems, those first paragraphs I cited at the beginning of this chapter struck a chord with my experience.[1] I was increasingly worried that many students might still not be offered the opportunity to excel. I was concerned that lack of high expectations and opportunity to experience challenging curricula might ultimately shape lives in ways that could be limiting and unfair. Moreover, I was deeply concerned that failure to support the development of critical literacy skills might condemn many to a life filled with discrimination and voicelessness far beyond their school years.

I must confess that my initial questions and observations about how to provide high-quality, equitable literacy experiences for all students were fairly simplistic. Eventually, as our teacher research group joined others from around the state through conversations sponsored by the Alaska Council of Teachers of English (ACTE) and the Alaska State Writing Consortium (ASWC), we had no choice but to interrogate our most basic notions about literacy.

I will always be grateful for having been in that place at that time. While the diversity we found in Anchorage schools raised one set of questions, as we looked beyond the boundaries of a city to examine the literacy needs of adolescents who were growing up in small Alaskan communities and villages scattered across a geographic area the size of the United States east of the Mississippi River, we were forced to confront questions more complex than we could possibly have imagined at the outset.

Prior to that moment, I had not stopped to think deeply about how my values so strongly privileged one knowledge tradition and one way of knowing. My unquestioned assumptions and biases dictated the particular selections of literature I valued and taught and the very Western-oriented approaches to rhetoric and composition I drew upon. Even my unquestioned assumption that literacy was a way to move beyond one's home community and into the world actually served to devalue the strong heritages of many of our communities.

Our statewide conversations, a mirror of those happening in many other parts of the country, were compelling, and they raised enormous concerns about how we could possibly achieve uniform expectations for all of our students without imposing a new form of inequity upon many. Mingled in these complex deliberations was an emerging sense that our personal and national definition of literacy was too limited in its scope. We came to realize that literacy—as we approached the final decades of the century—required the ability to not only decode and comprehend, but also to draw upon and use higher-order thinking skills; to critically analyze the meanings one makes, to question one's own interpretations and conclusions as well as those of others, and to situate understandings in relation to multiple contexts and issues (Myers). Moreover, we realized that holding all adolescents accountable to the same expectations would be futile if we did not also address their basic needs for equity in resources, experiences, and cultural/ethnic inclusiveness.

In Anchorage we had come to recognize that, while having high expectations for all students was important, that alone would effect little change if vital issues of equity and access to sufficient and appropriate materials, technologies, and services were not provided. For students who had no books at home, or no books written in a language they or their parents could read, access meant, among other things, providing essential materials. For students who entered school in the fall with particular needs for experiences, strategies, or supports, an equitable education must include sufficient opportunities to allow them to fully realize their potential. And, for true equity to exist, respect for diversity would have to result in inclusion of the stories and the cultures of all students. As *standards* came to represent high expectations, it became increasingly clear that for higher standards to succeed, we could never entertain notions of *standardization* in our interpretation or our delivery of them.

This distinction between standards and standardization proved to be an important one. And it is a distinction that I've noticed is not consistently made in the current discussion of school reform.

Moving toward National Standards

What are standards? And where did our national obsession with standards come from? A little history of the standards movement might help chart the course on which we now find ourselves.

In 1991, President George H. W. Bush and the nation's governors commissioned the National Education Goals Panel to address educational concerns. Emerging from this education summit was Goals 2000 which described as its mission:

> To improve learning and teaching by providing a national framework for education reform; to promote the research, consensus building, and systemic changes needed to ensure equitable educational opportunities and high levels of educational achievement for all students; to provide a framework for reauthorization of all Federal education programs; to promote the development and adoption of a voluntary national system of skill standards and certifications; and for other purposes. (1)

That same year, the Department of Labor released *What Work Requires of Schools: A SCANS Report for America 2000*. From the *SCANS Report* and the work of the education summit came Goals 2000. Goals 2000: Educate America Act proposed that by the year 2000, students graduating from American schools would demonstrate "competency over challenging subject matter including English, mathematics, science, foreign languages, civics and government, economics, arts, history, and geography."

It was in this climate that the International Reading Association (IRA) and the National Council of Teachers of English (NCTE) began the development of the Standards for the English Language Arts in 1992; in beginning this process, they embarked on a lofty goal:

> to ensure that all students are knowledgeable and proficient users of language so they may succeed in school, participate and contribute to our culture, and pursue their own goals and interests as independent learners throughout their lives. (NCTE Standards, 5)

This first national standards project was initially supported by a grant from the U.S. Department of Education to the Center for the Study of Reading at the University of Illinois to support work with NCTE and IRA. Though grant funding was withdrawn within two years, NCTE and IRA leaders decided to move ahead with their development project, establishing a four-year national effort that included literally thousands of teachers, administrators, policymakers, parents, and others in the most inclusive conversation ever held about literacy.

Not only did this broad-based effort emphasize a deeply rooted commitment that standards must be "grounded in what we know about language and language learning" (5), but it also placed enormous value on the importance of stakeholders talking and reasoning together. Three "core beliefs" provided a frame for these discussions. These included agreements that "standards are needed to prepare students for the literacy requirements of the future as well as the present"; that "standards can articulate a shared vision of what the nation's teachers, literacy researchers, teacher educators, parents, and others expect students to attain"; and that "standards are necessary to promote high educational expectations for all students" (2).

Instead of going the route of other national organizations which attempted to capture all the detailed knowledge that experts felt important in a discipline, the IRA/NCTE Standards for the English Language Arts (Figure 1.1) instead offered twelve interrelated standards that define the range of experiences and expectations for listening, speaking, reading, writing, and critical viewing. These standards were offered as *starting points* for curricular planning that could capitalize on the expertise and interests of teachers and students. Instead of being offered as prescriptions, these standards were intended to support conversations and planning at every level of instruction that could mirror the inclusive and dynamic nature of the national standards development process for English language arts.

With enthusiasm, I joined the thousands of others in national standards conversations. I believed in the strength and wisdom of this remarkable and vast collection of educators to sort out the weighty questions inherent in any contemplation of uniform standards and issues of equity. Finally, I thought, educators would have the strength of our national organizations behind us as we lobbied for changes that would improve the quality of literacy instruction for all students. Though teachers across the country were keenly aware of and continued to wrestle with the complexities involved in creating equitable and challenging standards for a diverse population, we nonetheless believed that collaborative work among dedicated English educators would lead to greater opportunity and a more level playing field that honored the traditions and needs of all students.

Each of the twelve national standards addressed a spectrum of literacy expectations that function as an umbrella, providing a framework of expectations. Instead of focusing on particular titles or authors, for example, standards one and two described a need to provide a wide range of experiences with texts that spans historical periods, authors, genres, media, and more. Within this range of textual experiences, the standards described equally ambitious and far-ranging strategies and purposes for text-based experiences.

Perhaps most significant, these standards demonstrated the two organizations' fundamental belief in the ability of teachers and other local stakeholders to make crucial decisions about best ways to meet the standards for remarkably varied populations. Building from the standards themselves, NCTE moved further to provide guidance for those who were responsible for implementation in three significant ways: through additional policy development, through extensive professional development, and through representative modeling of best practices.

Figure 1.1. The IRA/NCTE Standards for the English Language Arts

---

1. Students read a wide range of print and nonprint texts to build an understanding of texts, of themselves, and of the cultures of the United States and the world; to acquire new information; to respond to the needs and demands of society and the workplace; and for personal fulfillment. Among these texts are fiction and nonfiction, classic, and contemporary works.

2. Students read a wide range of literature from many periods in many genres to build an understanding of the many dimensions (e.g., philosophical, ethical, aesthetic) of human experience.

3. Students apply a wide range of strategies to comprehend, interpret, evaluate, and appreciate texts. They draw on their prior experience, their interactions with other readers and writers, their knowledge of word meaning and of other texts, their word identification strategies, and their understanding of textual features (e.g., sound-letter correspondence, sentence structure, context, graphics).

4. Students adjust their use of spoken, written, and visual language (e.g., conventions, style, vocabulary) to communicate effectively with a variety of audiences and for different purposes.

5. Students employ a wide range of strategies as they write and use different writing process elements appropriately to communicate with different audiences for a variety of purposes.

6. Students apply knowledge of language structure, language conventions (e.g., spelling and punctuation), media techniques, figurative language, and genre to create, critique, and discuss print and nonprint texts.

7. Students conduct research on issues and interests by generating ideas and questions, and by posing problems. They gather, evaluate, and synthesize data from a variety of sources (e.g., print and nonprint texts, artifacts, people) to communicate their discoveries in ways that suit their purpose and audience.

8. Students use a variety of technological and information resources (e.g., libraries, databases, computer networks, video) to gather and synthesize information and to create and communicate knowledge.

9. Students develop an understanding of and respect for diversity in language use, patterns, and dialects across cultures, ethnic groups, geographic regions, and social roles.

10. Students whose first language is not English make use of their first language to develop competency in the English language arts and to develop understanding of content across the curriculum.

11. Students participate as knowledgeable, reflective, creative, and critical members of a variety of literacy communities.

12. Students use spoken, written, and visual language to accomplish their own purposes (e.g., for learning, enjoyment, persuasion, and the exchange of information).

A quick visit to the NCTE website (www.ncte.org) provides educators and interested members of the public with extended policy documents that further define and explicate the standards. For example, the *NCTE Beliefs about the Teaching of Writing* (Figure 1.2) provides eight guidelines spanning research on all aspects of writing instruction and assessment. This document provides details to guide local conversations about the teaching of writing, and it has been used in the formulation of various state standards documents. Policy documents and guidelines are also available for many other major areas of English language arts, including those for adolescent literacy, included in the front of this volume and summarized inside the back cover.

Recognizing that new and evolving expectations for literacy will require that teachers acquire expertise in new strategies, NCTE has designed and hosted many and varied professional development opportunities for educators. While these include traditional venues such as national, regional, and state conferences, efforts also include Web-based supports such as Pathways, CoLEARN, Web seminars, chat rooms, and other electronic forums to support teacher conversations. An active professional development network brings outstanding presenters who address a host of literacy topics into local regions for workshops and institutes. A plethora of print materials—from journals and books to position papers and policy documents—provide examples and models of standards in action to help educators think about their own planning and implementation processes.

All of these efforts are significant because of the foundational messages they embody: Standards should lead the way and encourage informed local conversation and decision making. Standards are not prescriptions; they are guidelines that build from the best research in the field and represent a consensus of the best thinking of literacy leaders. They do not offer scripted approaches; they do not tell us what page to be on at a particular moment in the year; and they do not substitute for professional thinking and planning. Instead, they provide essential support. *Standards, in other words, are not the same as standardization.*

Figure 1.2. From *NCTE Beliefs about the Teaching of Writing*

---

1. Everyone has the capacity to write, writing can be taught, and teachers can help students become better writers.

2. People learn to write by writing.

3. Writing is a process.

4. Writing is a tool for thinking.

5. Writing grows out of many different purposes.

6. Conventions of finished and edited texts are important to readers and therefore to writers.

7. Writing and reading are related.

8. Writing has a complex relationship to talk.

9. Literate practices are embedded in complicated social relationships.

10. Composing occurs in different modalities and technologies.

11. Assessment of writing involves complex, informed, human judgment.

A Struggle of Metaphors

English teachers know well the power of metaphor. For many decades, our nation's schools have operated within a pervasive industrial metaphor indicative of the events going on in the culture as a whole. An entrenched ideology of part-to-whole approaches to learning were so deeply engrained in our post–World War II educational systems as to be largely unquestioned. It is this thinking that has promoted assembly line models of learning: breaking complicated literacy tasks down to their smallest parts, teaching and testing the parts, and eventually producing a shiny new high school graduate who would roll out of the school and into college or the workplace fully prepared for the challenges ahead.

It is important to recall that this industrial metaphor has not always been our prevailing notion for schools or for learning. Through much of our nation's history, the metaphor that guided thinking about schools was far more agrarian and organic. To sense the full impact of the difference in thinking, one might consider the stances of the farmer and that of the factory supervisor. Within the farmer's context, much must be considered. Deep knowledge of context, location, seeds, fertilizers, technique, skill, and craft is required to coax a crop from the earth. The farmer knows that some variables are within his control; others simply are not, though he can do some things to compensate. He might not be able to prevent a drought, but he might be able to provide needed extra resources through irrigation. Even accounting for his best planning, there are factors beyond his control. Though every seed might come from the same previous crop, meet the same standards for selection, and receive equivalent expert care, the production will vary.

In the farmer's domain, the notion of high standards enters at every level of the process. The farmer must know a great deal about selection of raw materials; about methods for planting, nurturing, and cultivating; about processing and marketing his product. The farmer works for and expects a high yield from all of his crops, and he sets high standards for his own work to produce a quality crop at the harvest. Though there are predictable steps in the process, nothing is prescriptive. Instead, it requires bringing the best research and knowledge to the task of growing the crop every day, making thoughtful judgments on a continual basis, and realizing that to achieve the high standards for performance he hopes for, he will be required to vary technique based on the conditions he confronts daily.

The farmer realizes that growing quality crops is a highly recursive process, one that requires careful and reflective practice across a career. Every crop is different. Crops in different fields vary in growth patterns. The strategies that work best with one set of circumstances may be less effective in another. The job of the farmer is to pay attention to the very complex and interconnected set of circumstances in play and to bring the very best professional expertise into practice day-by-day.

Think of the contrast to the assembly line. Certainly there are many thoughtful and professional judgments that have gone into creating the parts that will be assembled on the line. And yet, within the process itself, parts are parts. Each part is complete, perfect, and ready to fit into its allotted slot. If it isn't, it becomes part of the scrap pile to be melted down so that the process can begin again. In the assembly line world, it makes sense to break down processes to their smallest component, and each piece must do its function consistently. Quality control provides the testing to ensure that parts become bigger units, and these units all move from the line functioning in exactly the same way.

The contrast between agrarian and industrial metaphors is important in order to understand the struggle currently embedded in the nation's movement toward standards-based education. If standards have been conceived with an agrarian view, they provide guidance for educators who, in turn, draw upon their own professional and continuously developing knowledge to create learning environments that support the growth of all students. Within this metaphoric view, teachers realize the critical need to observe literacy learners constantly, drawing upon formative and summative assessments to better understand what their students are learning and how they might need to modify the lessons or content to better address learner needs. Implicit in this vision is the requirement that teachers be experts in their discipline and in their pedagogy. With this expertise, they become essential to the daily and long-term decision making that must take place if standards are to be translated into effective instruction for students. The IRA/NCTE Standards for the English Language Arts exemplifies this vision of literacy education.

What happens if the metaphor adopted is instead one of an industrial approach? I would imagine that schools would experience a push toward standardization. There might be an effort to treat all students as if they are the same, and, if by chance they come with different experiences, needs, or interests, to ignore those variables. Within that framework it would be logical to offer them the same program of studies, the same instructional materials and methods, and the same tests to determine how close to the target goal their achievement has come. It would certainly make sense to break down each process to its smallest parts, develop a recommended sequence for teaching the skills and, at the end of the process, assemble the entire "package" into a finished product: nouns and verbs one year, phrases the next, clauses later, until the student is ready for the moment when everything comes together in a self-actualized wholeness as manifest in the essay or the research report. Of course, we would want to test each new piece of knowledge along the way and check it off when the target level of expertise was attained. And conveniently, once a skill or bit of knowledge was checked off, learners could confidently move forward, knowing that this piece was permanently in place.

There is a bit of substance that is very alluring about the industrial model. As a new teacher, I was, in fact, convinced that isolated instruction within a sequence made sense. I recall vividly the week that I spent teaching seventh graders rules for using commas. Each day we explored one more grade-appropriate rule. I created worksheets that provided practice with commas in a series, at the end of introductory clauses, after complete clauses in compound sentences, and more. Students completed the worksheets and did amazingly well on the test that Friday. Grading the test over the weekend, I experienced that lovely moment of self-congratulation that so often precedes a fall! Come Monday, I discovered that the students had indeed learned something about commas. They seemingly had surmised as a group that their teacher loved commas, so they went home, filled salt shakers full of them, and commenced to sprinkling each of their various pieces of writing with a liberal dash over the next months. Though a painful lesson, I did learn once again that my students were not parts on an assembly line, that teaching even the most minute convention is a highly recursive process that is best learned within an authentic, integrated context.

Before moving on to consider how each of these metaphors is inherent in the standards that feed into the open funnel and, hence, into classrooms around the country, it is important to remember that American education has been intensely influenced by each of these metaphors during some point in our history. Prior to the twentieth century, we were far more rooted in an agrarian model for education than we are now. Along with the industrial revolution, the last century brought us assembly line practices that have influenced almost every aspect of education (Nehring, 425–432). Depending upon what happens with standards implementation in the next decade, that influence is apt to continue and possibly to intensify. That's why it is so essential that educators know what influences are in play, what beliefs are shaping the standards for their states, and, ultimately, how to situate themselves in the state and national conversation so that they can help shape standards that support adolescent literacy rather than hinder it.

Standards and Adolescent Literacy

More than a decade after the IRA/NCTE Standards for the English Language Arts were adopted and long past the establishment of Goals 2000, with its target that "every adult American will be literate and will possess the knowledge and skills necessary to compete in a global economy and exercise the rights and responsibilities of citizenship," literacy leaders continue to express alarm about the state of literacy among adolescents. *NCTE Principles of Adolescent Literacy Reform* (2006), the larger document upon which *Adolescent Literacy: An NCTE Policy Research Brief,* referred to in this volume, was based, opens with its own alarming announcement: "Over 8 million students in grades 4–12 read below grade level, and 3,000 students with limited literacy skills drop out of high school every school day" (2). Citing studies by ACT, this document goes on to report that "only about half of our nation's high school students are able to read complex texts" (2), and it describes the dire challenges facing under-literate adolescents as they move through and beyond K–12 schools. These are startling pronouncements, particularly in light of two decades filled with discussion and the adoption of policy, standards, legislation, and increasingly high-stakes testing for students.

There *is* much reason for concern. From our nation's earliest history, our leaders have cautioned us that we cannot maintain a democratic society unless we have informed, literate citizens. We have become increasingly aware of the impact of the new "flat world" described by Tom Friedman. Now more than ever, young people will face heightened competition in all aspects of their academic and economic lives.

As I noted earlier, definitions of literacy have shifted, and this is particularly true for adolescent literacy. Views of literacy as the ability to decode and comprehend texts and to write simple, coherent sentences are simply insufficient for the challenges facing citizens of the twenty-first century. For today's young people, literacy extends far beyond reading, encompassing "reading, writing, and a variety of social and intellectual practices that call upon the voice as well as the eye and hand" (*Adolescent Literacy: An NCTE Policy Research Brief*, 14). In school and outside of school experiences support the development of literacy as students interact in varying social settings, work with a host of media, and participate in an array of personal, family, and community activities. Teachers have a unique and vital role in supporting literacy development, but so do parents, friends, and a wide range of others with whom adolescents interact.

Today, we know a great deal about adolescent literacy, but unfortunately this research base is sometimes ignored. The current debate about standards too often falls victim to myths about literacy, defining, in very narrow ways, what students should know, where they gain literacy skills, and the purposes for which literacy skills are important. When all students are subjected to the same approaches, texts, and assessments without accounting for individual interests, strengths, needs, and preferred methods of demonstrating knowledge and skills, the good intentions of the standards movement slip dangerously off track as practices become standardized. What, then, do we know about adolescent literacy?

Adolescence represents a unique moment in literacy development. *Adolescent Literacy: An NCTE Policy Research Brief* describes literacy as encompassing all of the language arts, as an "ongoing and non-hierarchical process" (14) that is recursive, social, and unique to the task at hand. At this crucial crossroads, while continuing to develop their literacy skills, adolescents also rely heavily on literacy to engage in academic and social interactions. Students have acquired a level of comfort with particular literacies and disciplines, and the skills they exhibit as well as the choices they make are apt to reflect those comfort levels. Adolescents, as any middle or high school teacher can attest, are social creatures; they use their literacy skills as they engage home, peer, and academic communities, among others, for a wide variety of purposes. Standards that address only a narrow understanding of adolescent literacy are often doomed to failure.

Motivation, we also know, is key to adolescents' success and "can determine whether students engage with or disengage from literacy learning" (*Adolescent Literacy: An NCTE Policy Research Brief*, 16). Building motivation requires strategies that engage, challenge, draw upon past experiences, and encourage connections to current questions and interests; building these strategies will necessitate use of diverse texts and an emphasis on self-selection. Building comprehension must account for many traditional literacy skills but also include strategies to help students read their worlds, including the worlds made of diverse disciplines and filled with media-rich texts. Critical thinking promotes a stance that necessitates reflecting about one's own thinking—self-monitoring, interpreting, analyzing, using literacy across disciplines, and drawing upon technology in specific, thoughtful, and appropriate ways (6–7). If literacy education fails to develop motivation, comprehension, and critical thinking, adolescent learners will not be engaged, and our staggering concerns about adolescent literacy will continue to spiral.

Research on adolescent literacy has left few doubts about the importance of particular types of practices and suggests in the strongest possible ways the importance of particular types of standards. Standards should address essential questions about what all students should know about literacy and be able to do with literacy. What teachers, administrators, and policymakers do with standards must account for what we know about student needs and reflect the best pedagogy available. However, as I'll discuss in Chapter 2, not all standards that are funneled down to teachers reflect this deep understanding of adolescent literacy. As we examine other national standards in Chapter 2 that are influencing local classrooms, consider these two questions as a way to frame the discussion:

1. How do each of the various standards documents account for current research on adolescent literacy?

2. What values are represented by the standards that are included in each?

Note

1. *A Nation at Risk* signaled the beginning of a movement many see as igniting a crisis mentality about education. Berliner and Biddle, for example, talk about this clearly in their volume *The Manufactured Crisis*.

**Chapter
Two**

Will the Real Standards Please Step Forward?

*Our administrators told us that we have to show how we meet every
single one of the content expectations . . . all ninety-one
of them . . . each year. I've spent hours this year filling out forms to
prove what I've always done. Now, there's no time left for me to do new
planning. I'm just stuck filling out paperwork. . . .*
(Michigan teacher, 2008)

In the spring of 2004 when I was invited to chair the committee that would revise the high school English content expectations for the State of Michigan, I approached the task with caution. The state had entered the arena of standards development more than a decade earlier with a broad-based process that included educators representing all levels of instruction who came together to craft standards and expectations for student learning that reflected the highly integrated nature of the English language arts. That earlier work, used extensively by teachers and curriculum directors, had guided enormous curricular changes for more than a decade.

This new round of development represented a yielding by the state to pressure from some internal stakeholders and from a few powerful external organizations. To a substantial degree, both pressure groups shared a pervasive concern for the economic well-being of the state and nation, and both believed that education was critical to addressing their concerns. The Michigan Department of Education (MDE) conveyed upon our committee the charge of creating new literacy standards that would reflect world-class content expectations challenging enough to prepare *all* students for college ("Creating a 21st Century Michigan Workforce,") and with skills for the workplace. As chair of the committee, I was instructed that the majority of the committee membership must be university professors who were considered experts in their field of study—literature, writing, and communications—to ensure that the bar would be set high enough to achieve the world-class content standards envisioned for Michigan high school students.

This requirement was problematic for me and other committee members who bristled at the notion that university instructors were better suited to bring essential expertise to the task of standards revision. Of help was the fact that committee members possessed deep roots in secondary classrooms. Most of the members had been secondary teachers, and all of us worked extensively with secondary teachers and continued to work actively with secondary students as they transitioned to the university.

The committee as a whole agreed early on to a set of guiding principles that governed our work, including a commitment to honor the integrated vision of the earlier standards.

- We realized that standards and expectations were *not* curriculum documents, but that poorly written standards and expectations could do serious damage to curricular planning.
- We valued the careful ways in which successful secondary teachers structured instruction to capture important concepts before moving students into related but secondary bits of information.
- We recognized the importance of building upon existing student interests, areas of expertise, and motivation, and of extending these through pedagogies that connected students to new and challenging content—building confidence and investment as students venture into unfamiliar and more challenging texts and tasks.

Even before we examined and discussed standards and expectations produced by others, we determined that we wanted to create a document that supported the good pedagogies that we witnessed in classrooms of expert secondary teachers every day—instruction that built domains of knowledge and avoided a checklist of skills to mark off once they had been "covered" in class. In short, our primary concern was to develop standards that would effectively support adolescent literacy—viewed in all its complexity—across the state.

As we began our work we were directed to numerous important documents in the field and instructed to take them into account in our development process. We discovered that the new Michigan English content standards would be reviewed by several external groups, and it was understood that the standards we developed would be judged by these groups to be sure we had established sufficiently high expectations. Amazingly, NCTE and IRA were not among the external reviewers.

We read, discussed, and reflected on literally hundreds of pages of reform documents and standards, and came to realize very quickly how politically charged state and national standards development had become and how many voices had entered the conversation. For example, a quick Google search of the term *literacy standards* revealed more than 374,000 entries and suggested just how broad-based the involvement had become. These entries represent work from many different groups, reflecting distinct interests, assumptions, perspectives, and biases. In some cases, these efforts have focused on particular parts of the total literacy curriculum, drawing attention to specific standards and deepening our understanding of them. In other cases, organizations have worked to develop standards that are intended to specifically enhance workplace or business readiness skills, college preparation, or a common cultural literacy perspective.

Because standards developed by diverse groups have so directly affected standards at the state level, they have in essence directly entered the funnel that channels to the local classroom, likely contributing to the sense of confusion that many educators express as they move toward standards implementation. What became vital for our committee to recall—and what is equally important for teachers and administrators to realize—is that not all standards are created equal.

Standards inevitably reflect the interests of particular groups and—whether intentionally or not—imply particular views and beliefs about teachers and students. Understanding the mindset of groups that have produced such different expectations is imperative if educators are to make informed decisions about how they will read and use various standards documents. Gaining this understanding will help teachers and curriculum directors make judgments about standards, determine how standards relate to (or don't relate to) the abundant research on adolescent literacy, and establish a context for how standards and expectations are most appropriately addressed within the context of real classrooms.

One way to understand the complexity of these standards is to examine a few, looking specifically at examples from national disciplinary professional organizations and nationally and regionally influential, but not discipline-based, organizations. In the next section I look at two diverse sets of standards that have been especially influential in the creation of many states' standards, noting especially the perspectives each reflect and their influence on state-level decision making—and refer to several more that have gained in importance.

The College Board: *Standards for College Success*

Founded in 1900, the College Board is a nonprofit organization "whose mission is to connect students to college success and opportunity" (www.collegeboard.com, 2009). Those who initiated the College Board's entry into standards development believed that making college-readiness knowledge and skills explicit through standards would help to illuminate the pathway to college success for more students by "vertically align[ing] curriculum, instruction, assessment, and professional development in English language arts and mathematics across six levels beginning in middle school leading to AP and college readiness" (*Standards for College Success*, vi).

I was invited by the College Board in 2002 to participate in their initial standards development process, which eventually became Standards for College Success. The group of English educators who assembled in New York received a host of reports, research studies, and surveys to review. One, *Understanding University Success* (Conley), prepared by the Center for Educational Policy Research at the University of Oregon (with assistance from the Stanford Institute for Higher Education Research), described findings from a survey of more than 400 college professors who offered fairly traditional notions of what it takes to succeed in college. Other documents we reviewed described a variety of currently accepted practices and expectations (e.g., writing process, broad-based reading experiences, understanding that language changes in relation to varying rhetorical circumstances). The assembled members examined these materials, discussed observations from our own teaching, and explored research representing a variety of theoretical perspectives as we considered the knowledge, skills, strategies, and attitudes most vital to postsecondary success in English.

College Board leaders wanted each standard defined in terms of its content expectations, and then each of these expectations unpacked to fully define what students need to know and be able to do in relation to it at each grade level in order to successfully and sequentially navigate toward college entry and success. Ultimately, these very, very minute parts had to be aligned across grade levels so that it was clear how a particular skill progressed over six years of school at the secondary level. For example, five standards were developed for writing. These included:

Standard 1: Rhetorical Analysis and Planning

Standard 2: Generating Content

Standard 3: Drafting

Standard 4: Evaluating and Revising Texts

Standard 5: Editing to Present Technically Sound Texts

Looking at Standard 2 as an example, readers find two objectives:

W2.1: Student takes inventory of what he or she knows and needs to know.

W2.2: Student generates, selects, connects, and organizes information and ideas.

Drilling down further, for Objective W2.1 two performance expectations (PEs) are provided:

W2.1.1: Selects a topic, identifies what he or she knows about the topic, and determines the need for additional information.

W2.1.2: Identifies a variety of primary and secondary sources of information and uses a system for tracking sources.

Each of the various performance expectations was then further unpacked to show what is expected of the learner at each of six levels, corresponding to grades 6–12. As an example, for W2.1.1 one finds:

Level 1: Identifies an issue of personal interest, inventories and organizes what he or she knows about it, and identifies areas for further research.

Level 3: Transforms a working issue into a working thesis claim; identifies, organizes, and considers the relevance of known information; and determines the need for further research.

Level 6: Refines a working thesis claim based on his or her exploration and organization of existing information and consideration of various perspectives, identifying areas for further research.

Each of the objectives and performance expectations was then defined for four different types of writing: argumentative, research writing, literary analysis, and creative and reflective writing. (The performance expectations noted above are for argumentative writing.) Even a cursory glance at these expectations shows that traditional college writing genres such as essays, reports, and research papers were heavily privileged.

The goal for the development process was to make it clear what the College Board believed students would need to know and be able to do for success in college—in this case, traditional college essay writing. As one of the consultants to the project and one who approached the work from a teacher stance, I found myself frequently struggling as the development moved forward. Though prefatory materials carefully described the recursive, integrated, and interdisciplinary nature of writing, the level of detail used to describe processes that typically are thought of as wholes suggests a fragmented approach to teaching writing. Moreover, though the standards themselves followed a process approach to thinking about composing, the suggestion of a developmental sequence for highly recursive skills and strategies set forth an expectation that certain steps must always come before others, and that once students have accomplished a particular performance expectation, they can then check that one off and move on to more sophisticated ones. Finally, as is generally the case in documents such as this one, no "weight" is given to particular expectations; hence, all of the performance expectations are presented as equally important.

As with any standards, Standards for College Success has a particular focus and, as a result, represents many decisions at each juncture of development regarding what would be included and what would not be addressed. As noted earlier, the major value was placed on traditional college genres. Other parts of the standards address reading, literature, and, drawing heavily upon other standards developed by the National Communication Association, listening, speaking, and media literacy. The standards do not claim to be comprehensive, and this is important for classroom teachers and curriculum directors to remember. They may be helpful for defining aspects of particular genres of traditional college reading and writing, for aligning curriculum vertically, and particularly for preparing for particular types of assessments.

Standards for College Success eventually came to weigh in on the standards development in Michigan (and in many other states as well), as we were asked to use these standards as a benchmark for what should be included in the state's document. In Michigan, Standards for College Success was listed as a resource for teachers and school districts so that we did not need to replicate the very fine level of specificity it provided for particular academic skills. The College Board standards continue to raise many questions that deserve further investigation, particularly as teachers make critical decisions about the amount of class time that will be set aside to teach and reinforce particular academic genres at the expense of other reading and writing experiences.

Achieve, Inc.

Most secondary teachers are familiar with the College Board and ACT, but as I've worked with groups across the country, I've been surprised that so few know anything about Achieve, Inc. Created in 2002 by the National Governors Conference and national business leaders, this nonprofit, bipartisan group holds remarkable sway in determining which standards are included in state documents and what policies various states will pursue in terms of establishing graduation requirements and determining how students will fulfill them. In 2005, Achieve cosponsored the National Education Summit on High Schools; forty-five governors attended. In 2008 the organization reported that "[t]hirty-two states have joined with Achieve to form the American Diploma Project" and that Achieve had "helped more than half the states benchmark their academic standards, tests, and accountability systems against the best examples in the United States and the world" (*Closing the Expectations Gap, 2008*). In a very short span of time, Achieve has gained more power over state standards than any other group has ever exercised.

In 2004, Achieve released its own national standards for literacy and for mathematics in the American Diploma Project's *Ready or Not: Creating a High School Diploma That Counts*. The explicit goal for this document has been to align state standards with the proficiencies that Achieve feels students will need to be successful in college and the workplace. A total of sixty-two expectations define eight standards for English language arts.

As with all other groups, the standards created by Achieve represent a very particular focus, perspective, and set of beliefs. For literacy, these standards include:

A. Language

B. Communication

C. Writing

D. Research

E. Logic

F. Informational Text

G. Media

H. Literature

Looking at the Literature standard (H), for example, you'll find nine content expectations that provide focus for the literary experiences that all students should achieve. These include:

H1. Demonstrate knowledge of eighteenth- and nineteenth-century foundational works of American literature.

H2. Analyze foundational U.S. documents for their historical and literary significance.

H3. Interpret significant works from various forms of literature: poetry, novel, biography, short story, essay, and dramatic literature; use understanding of genre characteristics to make deeper and subtler interpretations of the meaning of the text.

H4. Analyze the setting, plot, theme, characterization, and narration of classic and contemporary short stories and novels.

H5. Demonstrate knowledge of metrics, rhyme scheme, alliteration, and other conventions of verse in poetry.

H6. Identify how elements of dramatic literature articulate a playwright's vision.

H7. Analyze works of literature for what they suggest about the historical period in which they were written.

H8. Analyze the moral dilemmas in works of literature, as revealed by characters' motivation and behavior.

H9. Identify and explain the themes found in a single literary work; analyze the ways in which similar themes and ideas are developed in more than one literary work.

In addition to the standards and expectations, two lists of recommended readings are included. From the Indiana state standards (standards that have been approved by Achieve and frequently used as a model of excellence by Achieve), explicit titles are provided for fiction (classic and contemporary), historical fiction, science fiction, folklore/fairy tales, mythology, poetry, short stories, drama, essays and speeches, and a variety of nonfiction texts. From Massachusetts, titles are provided for American and British/European literature, detailed by time periods and some genres (see www.achieve.org/node/331).

In *Closing the Expectations Gap, 2008* (Achieve, Inc.), the authors describe the persistent problems students face when their high school programs fail to fully prepare them for the world beyond the secondary setting, drawing a correlation between rigorous coursework in high school and the likelihood of completing college. The 2008 report notes that though all fifty states have standards, most need "to ratchet up standards to what is required in the real world, colleges, and universities" (1). The report describes the mission of the Achieve standards to "provide a foundation for decisions on curriculum, instruction, and assessment," and as a means to "communicate core learning goals to teachers, parents, and students" (1). Achieve seeks to provide a metric that can be used to guarantee consistency among standards at a state level.

A review of the Achieve standards reveals a strong emphasis on traditional rhetorical skills for writing and speaking; historically valued pieces of literature; literary devices and literary genres; and English language usage and grammar. States are encouraged to assess the knowledge and skills that are outlined in the standards for all students, allowing for demonstrations of learning beyond straightforward tests. Troubling to educators who value the developmental, workshop, and community-building aspects of the classroom is the encouragement for states to develop proficiency testing that encourages the practice of "testing out" of classes by demonstrating mastery of the core knowledge, skills, and strategies that provide the content of specific courses. This becomes even more vexing when one considers the impossibility of capturing mastery of many of the English expectations in a testing situation.

Of concern as well is the noticeable absence of public school educators on the Achieve board or outreach to the disciplinary professional organizations most closely associated with literacy. If we believe literacy is everyone's business, then certainly it is the business of teachers and professional organizations made up of literacy experts. If you are a teacher or administrator charged with the development and implementation of standards, I encourage you to consider both the perspectives that are represented in Achieve's standards as well as those which are absent. This is particularly important as the organization gains power as an oversight group that has the ability to require changes in decisions made by state standards development committees.

In the case of the Michigan English content standards, recall that the standards development committee comprised a group of content experts, mostly from the university level and representing various language arts disciplines. The standards and expectations we created were, in turn, reviewed by Achieve using standards that had not been previously approved by the leading content experts in the field—the International Reading Association, the National Council of Teachers of English, and the National Communications Association! I want to argue that for the Achieve standards to have validity as a metric for critiquing state standards, it is imperative that they be subject to content scrutiny by the professional groups most intimately aware of current literacy research, theory, and practice. It is also imperative that teachers and curriculum directors vigilantly defend standards that offer a comprehensive view of the English language arts, thus supporting adolescents in all aspects of their lives.

In a book such as this one, it isn't possible to review more than a few of the voices that have entered the standards development conversation. As we worked to revise the Michigan standards, the College Board and Achieve were only two of the powerful influences that shaped our work. While the College Board advocates college readiness skills and Achieve traditional academic skills for college and work, other professional organizations, such as the National Communication Association (NCA), have developed detailed standards that have been used by many states to develop their own standards for communication, listening, speaking, and media awareness (Figure 2.1). In addition, a wide range of documents coming from agencies such as the Department of Labor and the National Institute for Literacy, along with myriad policy statements and studies of all sorts, have all affected, directly or indirectly, the decisions made by state-level standards development committees.

Each of these sets of standards represents serious thinking by dedicated groups. Each also represents a set of perspectives and biases that envisions particular purposes, roles, and expectations for schools. Those charged with development of state standards must consider carefully the multiple, and often discordant, perspectives that weigh in upon their decision-making process as they craft bal-

---

Figure 2.1. Representative Voices That Influence Standards Development

---

- *Standards for Speaking, Listening, and Media Literacy in K–12 Education* developed by the National Communication Association (1996)
- *Secretary's Commission on Achieving Necessary Skills (SCANS) Report* (1991) issued by the U.S. Department of Labor
- *Equipped for the Future* (1995) issued by the National Institute for Literacy
- *Career and Employability Skills Content Standards and Benchmarks* (1998, 2001) developed by the Michigan Department of Education
- *Standards for College Success* (2005) developed by the College Board
- *College Readiness Standards* (2004) developed by ACT, Inc.
- *Literacy across the Curriculum: Setting and Implementing Goals for Grades Six through Twelve* (2004) developed by the Southern Regional Education Board
- *Understanding University Success: A Report from Standards for Success* (2003) developed by Center for Educational Policy Research
- *Every Child a Graduate: A Framework for an Excellent Education for All Middle and High School Students* (2002) developed by the Alliance for Excellent Education

---

anced standards that truly address the twenty-first century literacy needs of their students—and those teachers charged with implementing these standards should think about where these standards come from and what perspectives and biases they might represent.

Developing the Michigan English Content Standards

Of course, the standards development process in individual states reflects the unique circumstances and needs of each location. Nonetheless, the Michigan development process offers a representative example of much that occurs in standards development whether the locale is Alaska or Alabama or Arizona. In all cases, current standards development occurs within a context that requires attention to the many competing—and sometimes conflicting—expectations represented by, but not exclusive to, the examples discussed earlier in this chapter. All states face the responsibility of creating a framework of expectations that will support curricular decisions. These decisions will ultimately lead to course development that affects the futures of adolescents. The task is daunting, and the stakes are frighteningly high.

As our review committee made its way through hundreds of pages of materials generated by others, we found ourselves frequently asking questions. Do these various standards and expectations truly reflect the most essential knowledge and skills that all students need for literacy success in college and for jobs? Are particular expectations privileging certain cultural values and perspectives over others, and if so, do we have justification for those decisions? Are specific expectations relevant, appropriate, or valuable for students at the particular level under consideration? Certainly every set of standards and most of the reports and studies we reviewed helped us to solidify our thinking, though, of course, some were particularly valuable. Among the most helpful, not surprisingly, were the standards developed collaboratively by NCTE and IRA and those by NCA that specifically supported communications skills. In addition, various policy documents, including *Beliefs about the Teaching of Writing* and *Principles of Adolescent Literacy Reform* (both by NCTE), helped us to think about standards with an eye toward the students for whom they were developed.

As our work progressed we became intensely aware of how overwhelming standards and expectations could be. We decided on a structure that was intended to simplify this, clustering around four strands, then on standards, and finally on expectations that further defined the standards.

- Strand One: Writing, Speaking, and Expressing
- Strand Two: Reading, Listening, and Viewing
- Strand Three: Literature and Culture
- Strand Four: Language

Through many discussions and compromises, we ultimately defined these strands with fourteen standards that were ultimately explicated more specifically, resulting in a total of ninety-one content expectations (see www.michigan.gov). These standards represented the major areas for literacy study for all students and addressed essential elements such as writing process, reading and writing for varied purposes and audiences, and knowing that language use can and will vary based on rhetorical purposes. The movement to more finite descriptions was intended to offer teachers a definition of what should be considered across a program of study, not a prescription for what had to happen in a particular unit of instruction. This is an important distinction, and one we felt strongly about. Standards, not standardization, drove our work.

Michigan traditionally had been a state that left most decisions about high school graduation requirements to local districts. In fact, at the time the high school revision efforts began, only one course in civics was uniformly required for high school graduation across the state. Efforts to strengthen standards in core curricular areas were a part of a larger state process to raise graduation requirements for all students.

Within this framework of changes, we fought hard to maintain an approach that placed emphasis on local conversations and decision making, ensuring that all students would be privileged with a college readiness curriculum that was stimulating and also reflective of their interests and needs, and that decisions about how to address the standards would be made at the levels closest to local classrooms.

Just as in most other states, the revised Michigan content expectations for English language arts represented many compromises that resulted in a broad spectrum of learning expectations, including traditionally valued content requirements as well as a new emphasis on workplace literacy skills. For the latter, links were made to various documents that supported teachers as they considered the types of technical materials and broad-based nonfiction that should be included prominently in the curriculum. Eschewing layers of finely ground expectations, the committee chose instead to link the new standards to documents already available from other groups, including ones that had been reviewed as a part of the development process. For example, the College Board granted permission for a link to *Standards for College Success*, making that document readily available for teacher reference as desired.

Knowing the importance that was now placed on assessment and hoping to ward off the implementation of mandated statewide end-of-grade assessments that would, by default, lead to a state-imposed curriculum for grades 9, 10, 11, and 12, the committee devised the concept of locally developed common assessments. These assessments, intended to focus on common outcomes, were envisioned as a natural outgrowth of local curriculum planning and implementation and would allow school districts to create assessments that could be meaningful for teachers as they continually modified curriculum and for parents as they sought information about their student's progress.

As is so often the case, though the road to adoption of the standards was challenging, the path to implementation has been even more so. To our frustration, the message that was so central to our work—local development of curriculum based in these inclusive standards—has gotten somewhat lost along the way. For example, in the confusing communication to districts, some local administrators heard that each and every instructional unit that teachers designed would have to meet all ninety-one content expectations! Teachers, hearing such astonishingly impossible mandates, reacted with frustration and anger. Certainly some district administrators were more informed than others, but the spiraling miscommunication prompted the members of the standards writing committee to take an unprecedented step, creating an open letter to teachers in the summer of 2007 that explained in no uncertain terms the intent and design of the standards document (Figure 2.2).

The process of being so intimately involved in a state's standards development project has opened my eyes to some new understandings of the complexity of such an undertaking. In retrospect, the Michigan English content standards raise many issues that are universal in standards development, issues that are important for teachers charged with implementing the standards to understand.

Figure 2.2. Open Letter from Standards Writing Committee

TO: Secondary English teachers, principals, curriculum specialists, and the Michigan Department of Education

FROM: Authors and academic reviewers of the new High School Content Expectations: English Language Arts

It is an important and exciting time for high school English language arts in Michigan as the new content expectations we wrote and reviewed are now being implemented across our state.

Much good work on the part of teachers, administrators, and other educational specialists is helping to raise standards and expectations. The teaching of reading, writing, speaking, listening, and visually representing is being extended, deepened, and enriched in line with best practice in language arts research. We applaud these efforts to better prepare Michigan students for higher education and the workforce.

At the same time, reports we have heard from Michigan teachers about the implementation of the new language arts standards greatly concern us.

In some districts the language arts standards are being put into practice in rigid and restrictive ways, narrowing, rather than supporting, the freedom of local teachers to make decisions about curriculum and instruction. In some schools, the standards are being implemented without due respect for the complexity, diversity, and recursive nature of language arts learning. In some classrooms simplistic and uniform assessments are being put in place that undermine the authenticity and individuality of student learning.

Such practices were not the intent of the English language arts content expectations that we wrote and reviewed. Indeed, these practices may undermine the high expectations for rigorous learning set by the new standards and lower student scores on state-required assessment tests.

Learning in the language arts is highly complex, dependent on student interest, engagement, and relevant and meaningful immersion in language and culture. The teacher's content knowledge, interests, creativity, and passion are critical to guiding learning in our discipline. These understandings are crucial to the new Michigan language arts standards, standards far superior to the rote and simplistic standards found in some other states.

The new Michigan standards and content expectations should not be turned into check-off lists. Skills in writing, reading, speaking, listening, and visually expressing are not simply learned and then "checked off," as if that skill was over and done with. Instead, as the standards state, language arts skills are "recursive and reinforcing processes; students learn by engaging in and reflecting . . . at increasingly complex levels over time."

The new State of Michigan language arts standards do NOT mandate specific curricular content or literary works. No specific content or literary work is or will be required on state assessments of student learning in the language arts. The model curriculums that are provided by the Michigan Department of Education are sample and suggestive possibilities, but no school or teacher is required or expected to adopt these samples.

The standards are, in fact, designed to create the flexibility teachers need to create outstanding curriculum. In the case of Standard 3 literature, for example, teachers are urged to select from "a rich and varied selection of classical and contemporary, literary, cultural, and historical texts from American, British, and world traditions." Teachers are encouraged to utilize "a variety of literary genres representing many time periods and authors" and examples include "science fiction" as well as "myths and epics," "hypertext fiction," as well as novels" (3.2). Teachers are urged to draw on "knowledge of literary history, traditions, and theory" (3.3) as well as "mass media, film, series fiction, and other texts from popular culture" (3.4). Obviously, the standards are not intended to foster simplistic, "cookbook," or "one-size-fits-all" approaches.

Indeed, good curriculum is not static; it evolves with experience, new knowledge, and changing students. For example, given the particular background and interests of her inner-city students, a teacher in SW Michigan has developed an entire year language arts curriculum around *The Autobiography of Malcolm X*. Her curriculum addresses a series of vital issues raised by the book, including youth violence, racism, learning to read, social change, Islam, and world citizenship. It is tied to a range of relevant historical and popular cultural texts, and to a careful and extensive selection of other literary works with closely related themes. Although such a curriculum is not, at present, included as a "model," it fulfills a great number of the Michigan content expectations, and—more important—it is engaging and transforming the lives of students.

Figure 2.2. Continued

There are any number of appropriate and effective ways to organize curriculum: by theme, genre, nationality, period, ethnic group, or author. Given the diversity of students in many classrooms, it is often wise to teach multiple texts simultaneously, using literature circles, workshops, and individualized and independent instruction. It is also important to preserve a variety of pathways through four years of English studies, including focused elective classes that can play their role in helping to meet the variety of standards. The opportunity to dig deeply into a specific area or strengthen a particular skill is necessary to developing the in-depth thinking and mastery of tools necessary for college and workplace success.

While there are many stakeholders in the education of every child, it is each individual language arts teacher working in his or her own classroom who must, in evaluating their students, have the primary decision-making responsibility for implementing the new Michigan standards. As the standards document states, "Classroom teachers have extensive content knowledge, an ability to make on-going, data-driven curriculum decisions. . . . Teacher passion and creativity is essential to learning."

Throughout the new content expectations is the abbreviation "e.g.", from the Latin "exempli gratia" meaning "as an example." These examples are not mandates; they are suggestive possibilities to spur meaningful learning in the enormous range of Michigan classrooms. The standards we wrote and reviewed do not create a license for curriculum specialists at the state or district or building level to mandate content, curriculum, or assessment to classroom teachers. Instead, as the standards state, they are designed to "support conversations" that result in "rigorous and relevant curriculum."

As the standards state: "Students learn best by being actively involved in high-quality, challenging experiences; they demonstrate their learning best in authentic contexts. Not all skills are easily testable, especially on standardized tests; therefore, the curriculum must not be limited to teaching skills that are so tested." When students engage in content responsive to and extending their interests and abilities they will not only better learn language arts skills, they will develop the habits of reading and writing outside of school that are essential for skill development.

In some schools teachers are being asked to address all ninety-one content expectations equally in every language arts course. Instead, the standards state the exact opposite: "students and teachers are not expected to spend equal time on each strand or standard." It is highly significant that, unlike the K–8 standards, the high school standards are not written course-by-course or grade-level-by-grade-level, but instead create freedom and flexibility.

We wrote and reviewed the ninety-one content expectations with the clear understanding that each expectation was to be addressed at least once over the four-year high school span—not in every year or course. Many of the expectations will be covered multiple times, and others less frequently, decisions that can and should be made by teachers.

We are hearing of districts where teachers are being told that every student in every section of the same course should be on the same page of the same book at the same time, or that every section needs to have the same curricular units or the same assessments. Teachers simply cannot maintain high standards for all of their students if they are forced to give the same activities, assignments, or tests to everyone. This kind of standardization reduces learning for all and goes against both the spirit and the letter of the standards we wrote and reviewed.

The important challenge and significant role for districts is not to create "check-off lists" or "common tests," but to support teachers engaged in the challenging work of curriculum development, meaningful instruction, and authentic assessment. Teachers need time for collaboration, funding for new texts, and access to Internet resources. They need support for professional development, including graduate work, writing projects, and professional organizations.

The new standards should be leading to an outburst of new curriculums and approaches, as Michigan sets an example for the nation in high-quality, creative, relevant, rigorous, and engaging language arts teaching. Consider sharing your work and what you are learning from implementing the standards at the website http://www.mienglishstandards.com.

Michigan High School Content Expectations authors

(Co-signed by professors of English education throughout Michigan)

- Even good documents represent many layers of compromise. Lots of different groups have strong investment in particular aspects of curriculum. Standards documents provide a place for all those expectations to be expressed.

- Standards documents may need to consider purpose and audience in the same way that every other piece of writing does. The document that works for state policy or state test development may not (likely will not) be the same format that will be most useful to teachers for classroom planning.

- Multiple representations of what standards in action might look like will offer multiple visions of how to structure units of instruction in successful ways. Most of these representations should come from successful teachers who can share these with other teachers.

- Resources must follow new expectations. Teachers find it difficult to provide new experiences for students with no new materials or technology to support the curriculum. Professional development must be integral to implementation of standards. A piece of paper has never resulted in educational change—teachers have.

I know full well that expecting teachers who work with 150 students a day, every day, to read, absorb, and implement standards without assistance, resources, or support is simply unrealistic. So, what can a teacher do? How should a teacher read these standards? And what might teachers do to encourage sane implementation of standards in their own districts? In Chapter 3, as I look specifically at some of the challenges to standards implementation, I hope to spur some discussion at the local level about what teachers can do.

Challenges to Standards Implementation

Can you really tell me that all my students need to know all 91 of those expectations? I teach students who struggle to be in school at all. I'm not sure those standards have anything to do with my kids.

(Michigan teacher, 2008)

Two episodes that occurred within a single month forced me to revisit many of my concerns about the standards movement as a whole and the impact of standards implementation on local classrooms in particular. The first challenge was issued from the back of a large meeting room as about thirty-five teachers in a mid-Michigan professional development group came together to discuss their implementation efforts related to the new Michigan content standards for high school English. Like many other teachers in the State of Michigan at that time, they were frustrated . . . and some were angry. Despite the fact that the state standards and expectations represented outcomes for the entire high school program, these teachers had been mandated by their local district administrators to document how they were meeting all ninety-one content expectations—from classical British literature to memo writing—*in every unit they were teaching.*

Of course the requirement thrown before these teachers was impossible, and they had every reason to be furious. Fortunately, because I was a member of the committee that designed the standards, I was able to meet their anger with a bit of humor and a lot of facts about how the standards could and should be used. By focusing first on the strands and standards, we were able to talk about the intent of each standard and why each was both crucial for student success and, often, already a part of their instructional planning.

Maintaining our focus first on the forest, and then the trees, the teachers were not buried under the weight of ninety-one different expectations, making it possible to use their energy to reflect on their current practice, and to raise questions about what was working, how it was working, and for whom it was working. We could shift our discussion easily from considering how the standards were already reflected in their practice to entertaining how the standards could support the development of additional meaningful units of instruction that incorporated other important types of experiences and expectations that we would want students to experience.

Though that meeting ended well, I still drove home weighted down with the memory of the frustrated question: "why ninety-one content expectations?" Certainly, the standards revision committee had not started out with the plan to work until we had ninety-one! Instead, the content expectations grew organically as we collaboratively considered the scope of each of the standards; they were *never* intended to become a requirement on a list to be *covered* and *checked off*.

From the vantage point of the standards development committee, we believed one of the most significant values of the standards document would be the thoughtful reflection of educators as they considered the ways multiple standards interrelated to one another and related to various areas of curricular focus. For example, by first considering writing as a process and examining practice to determine how to help students gain a sense that all writing engages some sort of process, that these processes vary depending on many different factors, and that all writers have unique and recursive ways for approaching both new and routine written tasks, teachers would then be ready to entertain additional questions about process-based instruction:

- Are our students aware of the many different ways to generate and organize ideas and information? Do they realize that different strategies might support different approaches to writing in different genres?

- Do our students know multiple strategies for revising work including ones for looking at emerging texts sentence by sentence and paragraph by paragraph as well as others for macro-editing entire pieces?

- Are our students adept in getting and giving response to support ongoing development?

- Are our students careful with their selection of grammatical features and word choices appropriate to their choice of topic and genre? Which types of features should we most profitably focus attention on at a particular time to build those skills?
- Do our students grasp the intricate connections between writing and thinking? Between writing and reading or listening or viewing?

Working with standards in a *reflective* manner allows us to then step back and consider what might be missing, to focus attention on groups of students who may not be excelling, and to consider curricular changes that address newly identified needs. This holistic stance leads quickly to an approach that is far different from that which demands creating a unit oriented toward covering a list of skills embedded in content expectations—the very same approach that led to the frustration of teachers as illustrated by the concerned educators in my workshop.

The second episode, following closely on the heels of the first, forced me to circle back to the questions that encouraged my conversations with colleagues in Alaska years before regarding educational equity for all students. I had just returned from a walk with my friend Alice, a successful internist and one of the best-read women I know. On the television in her family room, a new game show asked adults questions from curricular materials designated for students in grades 1–5. "Name four demonstrative pronouns," the announcer asked. I teach English, so I quickly recalled *this*, *that*, *these*, and *those*. My friend, on the other hand, was not only stumped—she was frustrated. "I used to know that," she said with irritation. Then, "Why would I have to know that those words are called demonstrative pronouns to be smarter than a fifth grader?"

Good question, and one that relates to the convoluted path the standards movement has taken. At the onset of the standards movement, educators struggled to identify essential knowledge, skills, and processes that all adolescents need to know or be able to do to succeed in a fast-paced, global society. Soon, as we've seen, many other groups joined the conversation, attempting to capture and map all sorts of literacy information and processes deemed important within various disciplinary domains. In the process, I fear we have conflated two very different concepts: what is essential and what is possible. These are surely not the same thing. The fact that Alice failed to remember a grammatical term had no bearing on her adult literacy achievement or literacy behaviors. Certainly it would be grossly unfair to make any judgment about her literacy based on such a question. And yet for adolescents, far too many curricular documents and tests designed to measure literacy *do* make judgments based on items of this type. Perhaps it is time to consider once again what is essential for all literate adults to know and be able to do?

Alice's reaction to the television show mirrors the frustration I've heard expressed by educators in many parts of the country when a barrage of expectations have led to a Trivial Pursuit approach to curriculum that has encouraged an emphasis on isolated and easily forgotten details instead of deep learning of essential knowledge, strategies, and skills. As recipients of these varied expectations, teachers often have been left buried under a mountain of discrete skills, making it is easy to lose sight of what our own professional training and best practice tells us.

"Don't lose sight of the forest for the trees!" My grandmother would often remind me of this maxim when I allowed myself to become so caught up in details that I temporarily lost sight of the goal for a project. Too often the maps provided by standards have been less than useful to teachers because they are written to meet agendas that are not instructional.

Assessment efforts, for example, that find it easier to test straightforward bits of information instead of complicated literacy behaviors have prompted standards documents that reduce literacy to finely sliced fragments of information that are easily tested but essentially useless and often confusing for instructional planning. Too often, teachers have received standards that represent an amalgam of perspectives and multiple levels of administrative interpretation that encourage practices that are disturbingly reductive, hopelessly superficial, and sadly less inspiring than they should be. When this happens, standards might easily come to represent prescriptions to be resisted, not possibilities to be used as a platform for collaboration and planning; and, if this happens, creative teaching suffers.

What Do We Find When We Focus on the Forest?

First, as noted in Achieve's *Ready or Not*, expectations across multiple standards documents *do* reflect remarkably consistent patterns. We find an emphasis on writing and speaking that supports communication for a variety of purposes and audiences and in varied forms and genres. Most call for substantial engagement with reading, including many types of texts that represent varying authors, purposes, perspectives, and language choices. We find a greater awareness than ever before of the importance of connecting secondary literacy experiences with those of the "real world" that waits beyond high school, whether that be college or work or—as for most—both. Almost always we see strong expectations that all students will gain familiarity with Standard American English, though generally encouragement is also found for a broader exploration of the use and power of particular language choices. And generally we find strong encouragement to broaden the canon by offering students experiences with technical, informational, and historical texts as well as genres of writing that are found in workplace and governmental settings.

We also need to remember this: Standards provide a definition of what is possible, but *standards are not curriculum documents*. Looking at the forest requires that we make some hard decisions about what knowledge, strategies, and skills are most essential for *all* students at each point in their school experience. Knowing about rhyme schemes found in the works of eighteenth century British poets might be valuable. So might be understanding the specific literary devices and the balance and flow of a finely composed essay. The question for curriculum becomes one of balance and choices. How do we, as teachers, balance essential learning with cultural literacy? What approaches are most successful and efficient in helping students connect new learning to old, to use new skills as a path toward self-discovery of additional ones? How do we help adolescents develop frameworks and schema for remembering and contextualizing current knowledge, for pursuing new questions, and for analyzing new and potentially conflicting information?

Looking back to the research conducted and collected by experts in literacy and literacy instruction can also help. *Adolescent Literacy: An NCTE Policy Research Brief*, for example, offers a metric for teachers, school programs, and policymakers to use as they consider curricular changes that will promote excellence. The document summarizes what we know from programs that have demonstrated notable success with adolescent literacy instruction. These programs:

- emphasize developing the knowledge, skills, and strategies that allow students to become self-motivated, self-monitoring independent learners;
- draw upon a wide variety of approaches;
- focus on providing experiences with diverse texts, intensive writing experiences, strategic tutoring, technology, and text-based collaborative learning, among others;
- use direct and explicit instruction as appropriate, seeking to make visible the strategies proficient readers, writers, speakers, and listeners know and use;
- demonstrate an understanding that learning in the language arts is less sequential than recursive and developmental; and
- use formative assessments to hone instruction, and they shape summative assessments to reflect the desired learning outcomes for students.

Looking at the forest tells us this: successful literacy instruction is dependent on far more than standards (Figure 3.1). Teachers who are knowledgeable and engaged professionals are the *most* important factor in the improvement of adolescent literacy. Moreover, successful literacy instruction is also dependent on informed policymakers who deliberately align expectations and support for the classroom and place strong emphasis on supporting teachers in the development of carefully articulated programs that reflect the developmental and recursive nature of language arts learning.

Figure 3.1. Focusing on the Forest

Excellent literacy programs encourage:

- writing and speaking for varied audiences and purposes representing many different genres and forms;
- engagement with reading of many different types of texts representing varying authors, purposes, perspectives, genres, and language choices;
- focus on lifelong literacy and connections between school-based literacy and family and world literacies;
- conscious choices of particular language features, including Standard American English, for particular purposes;
- instruction in strategies to promote independent literacy pursuits; and
- classroom instructional time devoted to real reading and writing.

We also know that to promote deep learning, care must be given to contextualize discrete pieces of information within holistic and authentic processes, helping students gain power as lifelong learners who can communicate with varied audiences for many different purposes and in many different forms. Developing skills in critical reading and interpretation of varied texts; strengthening communication and information acquisition skills to support a lifetime of ever-changing needs for listening, speaking, and media literacy; and developing a critical stance that supports the ability to find and use information—these become priorities for instruction.

Time in the instructional day is precious. Because standards documents themselves are not adjusted for purpose and audience, the expectations that have poured into classrooms have sometimes promoted a fragmented "to do list" that may have a negative effect on instruction. Starting with a plethora of performance/content expectations can make unit development a dizzying prospect. At its worse, fragmentation of performance expectations could lead to a checklist approach to teaching. However, if standards are used as a means to help educators focus on the most important knowledge, skills, and processes that all students need, they can offer extremely helpful guidance in curricular planning.

It is important to keep in mind that our country has redefined its expectations for literacy many times as the needs of society have changed. Today, our needs encourage a level of literacy that is more sophisticated and challenging than ever before, requiring new training for teachers, new instructional strategies, new thinking about the skills and knowledge that students need, and new ways of assessing what students know and are able to do (Myers). Sadly, some of the policy decisions made in response to these needs have failed to produce the results intended by legislators and those who implement decisions at the national, state, and local levels.

Despite its alarmist tone, *A Nation at Risk* proudly described the fact that American schools "now graduate 75 percent of our young people from high school" (2). According to the National Center for Public Policy and Higher Education, "That figure has now dropped to less than 70 percent, and the United States, which used to lead the world in sending high school graduates on to higher education, has declined to fifth in the proportion of young adults who participate in higher education and is 16th out of 27 industrialized countries in proportion who complete college" (Fiske, 2). We can ill afford knee-jerk policy response to the very real issues surrounding adolescent literacy.

Clearly, improving literacy for all adolescents is an enormously important goal and one embraced by educators at all levels. As we pursue this goal, however, it remains critically important that changes be made thoughtfully and with keen attention to the immediate and long-term impact on adolescent learners. Equally important is the need to recognize that high literacy standards exist in classroom practice now. Drawing attention to successful instructional behaviors may support reflection on how similar practices might be extended to more students.

If standards are to achieve even a portion of their early promise—and I still believe this is possible—educators everywhere must consider carefully the role of standards in curricular planning, and collectively we must avoid being bogged down in an assembly line approach to covering expectations that fails to fully account for the organic and fluid instruction that good teaching represents. Again, standardization and standards are *not* the same. In the next chapters, I look closely at representative teachers and school districts to observe different ways they are raising the level of rigor in their literacy classrooms for all students. In each case, though standards are high, delivery systems vary, texts vary, and choices of projects vary. Drawing from a wealth of professional knowledge and an awareness of expectations defined by standards, these teachers practice the art of teaching as an ongoing professional inquiry.

2 Standards and Instructional Excellence

I sat with a small group of teachers from relatively affluent schools located within an intermediate school district just north of Detroit. As we discussed their implementation of the new Michigan high school English standards, focusing on the standards first before getting into the details of the content expectations, one of the teachers ventured, "Well, this doesn't seem so big a deal. I'm doing most of this stuff in my classroom already." Of course she was. As she discussed the units she had brought to this workshop, the International Baccalaureate program that she was helping design for her school, and the work she had done to bring many Advanced Placement strategies into all of her classes, it was clear that she is a thoughtful, professional, and dedicated teacher. Certainly the new standards would have a ring of familiarity to her.

The reaction of this teacher is not unlike those I've heard from many others. And, the reaction makes perfect sense. Well-crafted standards include knowledge and wisdom of outstanding teachers as a foundation to the development process. Well-crafted standards also mirror current research and reflect current literacy demands as recognized by leaders in the discipline who share their work through publications, workshops, and more. Such a wealth of information could be overwhelming and bewildering, but fortunately standards documents tend to reflect some commonly held visions of what all adolescents need to know about and do with literacy to become successful participants in varied literacy communities.

Teachers who are professionally engaged and dedicated to continually developing and honing their own practice, who strive continuously to learn as much as they can in order to meet the varied academic needs of their students, bring to standards development the wisdom and expertise of seasoned professionals. Because of their own professional engagement and personal learning, when they implement standards they do so within a context of ongoing research in their discipline as well as their own understanding of the needs of adolescent learners. For these teachers, standards can't lead to standardization, because they know full well the importance of differentiating instruction to promote success for the diverse students who populate their classrooms. They observe the patterns within multiple expectations and quickly assess how various expectations will fit into the integrated whole of instruction.

Standards should not feel foreign even if the genre in which they are presented to teachers sometimes appears that way. In Part 2, I invite you to enter the instructional worlds of teachers. We will look inside different types of settings and unpack instruction to examine how teachers in schools have worked with standards—as a map for possibilities, not a series of prescriptions. We'll look first at Nadine, a preservice teacher who struggles to work within an atmosphere of prescriptive standards-based instruction in her host school district, and I'll frame her frustrations within a new context of how things might be done differently by observing a more organic approach to standards implementation in a methods setting. Then we'll move on to engage two different groups of teachers in two very different settings—University School District (USD) and Mid-State School District. In USD, teachers approached the task of implementing new standards from a solid base of rich professional growth over time. These teachers were well informed about good literacy practices, and their needs for support in this process were far different from those of the teachers at Mid-State, where professional development had not been so readily available. In both cases, the movement from standards to the implementation of rigorous standards-based curricula was a messy and intense process that varied based on the strengths and needs of the teachers. And, as you read through the emerging unit plans and assessments offered, notice how the teachers came to realize that they have the power to affect the outcome of policy implementation. This section will lead us toward the final part of the book, which outlines plans for collaborative professional development and curricular planning to continuously raise classroom standards.

Adolescent Literacy through Standards-Based Planning

Chapter Four

"How has your first week been?" I asked Nadine, expecting to hear her usual rush of excited reporting. Instead, the light in her eyes dimmed and, with a sigh, she responded, "not so good." As I listened to her disappointed description of her first week of student teaching, of how she had received fully scripted units of instruction that she had to teach, and of how her students would be tested with the same assessments given at the same time for all the classrooms in her grade level, I felt my own heart sink as, once again, I confronted the sad reality that implementation of standards can be the single most deadly influence on adolescent literacy.

In universities around the nation, English educators work hard to equip preservice teachers with critical content knowledge in the various language arts disciplines—literature, writing, linguistics, and more—as well as knowledge about the research and theory that drive successful pedagogy for adolescent learners. As a student at Eastern Michigan University, Nadine had distinguished herself academically as one whose excitement about learning and teaching was impossible to miss. Filled with energy and passion for her own learning, she also had invested many hours in her methods classes practicing ways to bring creativity to her work with adolescents as she fashioned integrated units of instruction that built literacy skills supported by technology, a wide variety of literature, writing, and oral language experiences, service learning, and many more authentic learning experiences.

One week into her teaching experience, Nadine stood before me with a defeated tone in her voice, questioning whether her decision to teach high school had been the right one after all. Her commitment to her future students had not waivered, nor had her interest in her subject area. What had changed was her vision of the role she would be allowed to play in the classroom. For the first time she glimpsed the possibility that her vision of herself as a professional educator might not be welcome at the secondary level.

For Nadine, the first week in student teaching had been consumed with orientation to the required units that she would teach for the semester. Two novels had been selected for the term, and detailed, scripted lessons—right down to the required worksheets—were provided for her to use. Even the assessments were already developed and included. Though she had some latitude regarding which exercises to use and how much she would stress certain points within daily lessons, the fact that externally developed tests would be given at predetermined times left her fearful of leaving anything out lest she not stress information that students would encounter on them. Her job, she had been told, was to prepare her students for the tests which had been aligned with the state standards and with the high school exit exam made up of the ACT and a timed writing assessment.

Nadine apparently was not the only one awash in confusion, disappointment, and anger as a result of the week of inservice that preceded the fall semester. Her cooperating teacher and the other English teachers in the department, veterans with years of experience, appeared perplexed by the sudden imposition of required units that essentially disregarded their knowledge of content and of student needs. Like Nadine, they observed that scripted instruction left no place for them to function as professional educators. As I listened to Nadine detail the events of the week and looked over the materials she brought with her, I realized once again that good ideas can result in dismal implementation when instructional decisions are made in isolation from teachers who know so much about adolescents and adolescent literacy development and who are not allowed to bring their own passions and creativity to the planning.

The vision behind the new standards in Michigan aimed to enhance the professional decision making of teachers and improve literacy instruction, building upon themes or other organizing concepts, using a variety of fiction, literary nonfiction, and technical texts to support student learning that was rooted in real questions, authentic learning opportunities, and personal connections. The standards were constructed with a strong belief that teacher expertise, interest, and decision making are critical to the vitality and authenticity of the classroom learning experience of adolescents. Central to this vision was the commitment that the teacher must provide essential insight into the types of literature that would connect with individual adolescent lives and draw young readers into a rich body of texts, representing many different genres from across the centuries and from varying perspectives—literature that offers up accounts of how others have struggled with the same questions and issues that affect young adults today.

Somehow, however, the vision morphed in some districts into prepackaged units and even the kind of pacing guides Nadine was experiencing. How did this radical revision of our intention occur? In part, it seems to have grown out of good intentions. With the adoption of the new high school standards for English, the Michigan Department of Education decided to invest funding in sample units of instruction to be made available to local school districts for teacher support in curriculum development. These sample units, provided as models, were intended as an opportunity for teachers to see how other instructors envisioned addressing the standards across lessons, units, and grade levels. Used in this way, these units reflected recognition that the emphasis of instruction should not be on particular titles or authors, but on the outcomes desired for students. Such a vision for instructional planning, it can be argued, empowers teachers and curriculum directors to build diverse curricula that can be changed readily in response to student and community needs while still teaching the same standards and expectations to all students.

However, the reality has been that a number of districts have adopted these model units wholesale, presenting them to teachers as the new curriculum. The resulting vision of a classroom that is better served by mandated, predeveloped units, scripted lessons, and externally developed assessments represents, however, a jarringly different classroom from the one envisioned by the developers of the Michigan literacy standards. Instead of being a support to teacher planning, prescribed units represent a belief—however innocently—that teachers cannot be depended upon to develop high-quality standards-based units themselves. And the notion that teachers can simply follow the plans, stay on schedule, and prove that students have learned the essential content others deem important engenders a sense of dissociation from the day-to-day joy of teaching that keeps teachers and students engaged in the vibrancy of learning, replacing it instead with a factory-line approach that has brought such questionable results in the past.

Unfortunately, both new teachers like Nadine and veteran teachers such as those in her newly adopted high school found themselves equally stunned when confronted with an approach that does not trust them to develop a curriculum that meets high standards, and they responded in predictable ways—investing valuable time and energy creating strategies for resistance and questioning whether they have a place in a public education bent on depowering them and their students. Fortunately, it doesn't have to be that way.

Moving toward Standards-Based Teaching

Vignette 1: Understanding Standards in the Preservice Setting

I often teach a senior-level methods class that preservice students take immediately prior to student teaching. As a part of this class, I prepare students to create multiweek, integrated units of instruction that reflect the state standards for which they will soon be responsible. They know a great deal about standards before they arrive in my classroom. They have observed extensively in secondary settings, worked alongside excellent secondary teachers, and taken classes in lesson design, assessment, and more. In fact, by all accounts they are very prepared to begin the exciting process of developing their own instructional plans. Yet for many the idea of conceiving and designing an evolving unit that addresses multiple state standards in an integrated fashion is daunting and, for some, even a bit frightening.

To set the stage for their own planning, I choose to view with them snapshots of instruction from real classrooms where teachers thoughtfully weave an instructional tapestry that demonstrates practical and engaging practices for diverse student populations. We then carefully unpack the teaching episodes, paying particular attention to the standards—and later the content expectations—we see demonstrated. A final step is to discuss in small groups, and then as a whole class, ways that the lesson or unit might be enriched or redesigned to be more reflective of the new Michigan state standards before we begin to think together of logical focus points for their own units.

A series of tapes produced by the Educational Development Center (Michigan) with support by Michigan State University (1993) has proven to be particularly useful. Once we get past the giggles about changes in hair and clothing styles from a decade and a half ago, the tapes bring us directly into classrooms being taught by excellent teachers.

In the first tape we observe a remarkable educator from Saginaw, Michigan, as she guides her class through a discussion of Henrik Ibsen's *Hedda Gabler*. My students are asked to make notes of their own observations as they view the video: What do you notice? What do you see that reminds you or connects you to issues of instruction that you have studied in this class or elsewhere? What surprises you? What do you question? The lesson we view provides a snapshot from an involved unit that takes places over multiple weeks. As the video opens, we find ourselves in

Figure 4.1. Coming to Terms with Standards

- Observe examples of good teaching.
- Reflect upon the qualities of observed: what did the teacher *do* to create successful literacy instruction?
- Discuss with peers the practices identified and relate to the state content standards.
- Share with a larger group to fully develop the observations of good practice.
- Consider examples of similar good practice from our own high school experiences. Relate these to the new standards.
- Identify specific ways in which the instruction could be enhanced to more fully reflect new standards and expectations.

a traditional high school classroom; students sit in clusters scattered throughout the crowded space. My students notice immediately that the teacher is the only non–African American in the classroom, and I can see notes being made that may prompt later discussion (Figure 4.1).

In the first video my students and I watch, the scene opens with the high school teacher, Mrs. Smith, explaining to her students the expectations for the day. They are to read a portion of *Hedda Gabler* in small work groups, with each student assuming a part. Following their reading, the high school students have a series of response questions that are structured to take them into and beyond personal response. Ultimately, they will discuss the response prompts before working together to rewrite parts of the dialogue in contemporary language. By most accounts, this work represents a challenging reading choice. Ever since its nineteenth-century introduction, *Hedda Gabler* has sparked diverse responses—from stark ridicule to high praise—and the high school students readily accept the challenges the reading presents.

Around the room, clusters of students begin reading the assigned passages. Each student takes a part. Some struggle with the reading, stumbling a bit as they offer up their lines. The interdependence of the dialogue seems to help. Occasionally, one peer will help another if the reading becomes too difficult. They sometimes back up and reread a line or two, laughing a bit at funny parts as their understanding of the humor begins to emerge. Everyone is engaged in the sharing of lines—reading as their parts come up, listening carefully to one another, and talking a bit about particular phrases if they fail to understand what a character might mean.

Soon the students move to a list of prompts. Their instructions are simple. Based on the reading and on their personal understandings, they are to respond to each prompt and discuss these responses in their small groups. The camera takes us from group to group as we hear students tackle open-ended questions such as:

- What do you think this passage is about?
- What are the characters saying and why do you think they are saying these things?
- What's happening in the scene? Why do you think this is happening?
- If this play were being written now, what might the characters be doing to demonstrate these same ideas or actions?
- Has your opinion of Hedda changed as a result of your reading and discussion? If so, how has it changed?

Students start with their own reactions, jumping into the discussion with observations about Hedda and her behaviors. Some are quick to judge; some are intrigued by her coyness and the multiple layers of her desires and needs. Others focus more immediately on the male characters, and some are very critical of them in their relationship to Hedda.

As the high school students continue their small-group discussions, we see them repeatedly moving back to the text.

"I saw that here."

"Let me check that. . . ."

"No, um, I'm not sure that's what she said. Let me look for that."

Various responses and questions take students repeatedly into the text, and those textual visits produce additional information and insights that become part of the evolving discussion. Even in the quick snippets of conversations that we heard, it was clear that moving from personal response to group consensus supported by repeated readings took students to a deeper and more commonly shared understanding of the text. And, in some cases, it led to the development of questions that were more sophisticated than the ones that might have been raised by a solitary reader.

Once students had an opportunity to share the dramatic reading of the text, discuss in small groups their understanding and interpretation with supportive prompts, and revisit the text as needed, they reconvened to a spirited whole-class discussion. Here again, it was clear that the teacher was well prepared with carefully considered discussion prompts, but she seemed very at ease moving in a freewheeling fashion in pursuit of questions raised by students.

One group of students noted that Hedda sends mixed messages. "It's like she was saying no, but she was really saying yes." Another observed that Hedda never gets beyond being totally selfish, an interpretation that provoked both supportive and contradicting comments from other student groups. One student interrupted with an observation based directly from the text: "On goes the train . . . ," a comment that opened the door to many connections between the events of the text and those of contemporary society, raising questions about how much progress has actually been made in regard to complex gender issues.

As the class came to an end, the teacher reminded her students that they would be in the same groups tomorrow when they would try their hand at rewriting the script, translating it to the language of the present. This was the cue for my class to begin our own discussion. Only later, in our next class, would we establish a larger context for the unit we have just watched; then, as the tape continues, we will hear a discussion that includes three teachers, including Mrs. Smith, as they discuss their collaborative unit planning. For now, I'm interested in my students having a chance to process what they have observed.

"In your own small group," I instruct, "discuss what you noticed in this lesson."

My students immediately begin to share, noting the ease with which this teacher manages her classroom, the level of engagement of her students, the ways in which she moves students seamlessly from one activity to the next within a relatively brief class period, and how this variation in activity seems to help maintain student attention and involvement. Students observe that regardless of the activity, the focus on the literature is firmly maintained. As we move from our intimate, smaller groups to our whole-class discussion, sharing expands our picture of the various things that happened in the classroom and the many ways that Mrs. Smith skillfully orchestrated the learning process and content for her students. Of course all observations are not positive. We note that some of the adolescents stray sometimes; some groups wander off topic. Overall, however, even these events support the preservice teachers in identifying strong teaching behaviors and help them see how a skillful educator actually uses the many strategies and techniques they have learned in their university classes.

Building upon their observations, I nudge my students to begin thinking about the various teaching practices we have either witnessed in the video or found suggested by the teacher's comments. These preservice teachers are knowledgeable about writing process theory and pedagogy, about practices that encourage reader response and the use of other critical lenses for connecting and responding to literature, and about multiple strategies for engaging adolescents in meaningful reading and writing experiences. They have the advantage of having read from the works of Rosenblatt, Graves, Wilhelm, Appleman, Atwell, Romano, and many others whose work has shaped, and continues to shape the collective thinking within our discipline. This background helps the future teachers identify quickly ways that Mrs. Smith supported adolescents in:

- creating an interactive experience with a text—reading it, hearing it, discussing it, and translating the human interaction in it—as they engaged in individual and collaborative meaning making through recursive response;

- practicing critical reading and listening skills;
- using writing process to reflect, to analyze, and to translate language in order to promote comprehension and analysis of the text;
- developing awareness of language and the power that lurks in a word, a phrase, a gesture; and
- developing a keener sense that words and symbols on a page represent carefully considered choices made by a writer.

I selected this video to help my students establish a context for thinking about standards differently. My goal was to help them use an example of good, research-based practice as a frame for examining what standards may be asking of them. Instead of a collection of demanding expectations, I want them to see standards as a description of what an excellent teacher actually does on a day-to-day basis.

In another video snippet that we watch together, we observe Mrs. Smith planning in collaboration with two other colleagues. In this segment we learn more about how she builds context, how the lesson we have observed links with others that teach students essay writing skills that use writing process approaches. We hear more about the skills and strategies instruction that is woven throughout the unit.

Once we have taken the time to consider this sample lesson as an example of theory into practice, we shift our focus to the way it exemplifies the Michigan state standards, as well as standards set forth by NCTE/IRA. We recall that the multiple standards documents emerging from various constituent bodies hold certain expectations in common. Based on the two taped segments that we have watched, we observe that Mrs. Smith strives to introduce her students to an array of high-quality literature. The various strategies that she has drawn upon support personal and collaborative response, aesthetic and efferent reading experiences, connections to her students' own lives, and connections with other pieces of literature—all addressed in NCTE/IRA standards 1–3; in the Michigan state standards (2.1) strategy development, (2.2) making meaning beyond the literal level, (2.3) independent reading, (3.1) close literary reading, (3.2) reading and response, and (3.3) text analysis; and core to *Adolescent Literacy: An NCTE Policy Research Brief.*

Though we have not been able to witness a great deal of extended writing due to the brevity of the video, we have observed students using writing for a variety of purposes, including writing to learn and writing to reflect. And we know that they will use writing to translate part of the play's dialogue into their own language, a task that will require careful attention to language use in the past and language use in the present (NCTE standards 4 and 9; Michigan standards 4.1 and 4.2). In addition, we learn that students have written one or more essays during the course of the unit and that the essays already have been returned more than once for refinement.

Nearly all state standards place value on writing in a variety of genres for varying purposes and audiences. We learn in the planning video that the teachers' plans include multiple opportunities for students to translate their learning (e.g., an argumentative essay, a traditional literary essay, a persuasive letter to the teacher, a translated script, various reflective writings, and more)—addressing in complex ways NCTE standards 4, 5, 6, 7, and 9, and Michigan standards (1.1) writing process, (1.2) writing for personal growth, (1.3) purpose and audience, (1.4) inquiry and research, and (1.5) creating finished products. As a part of the various meaningful tasks completed in the unit, students build both technological skills and their ability to use Standard American English as described in NCTE/IRA standards 6, 8, and 12, and Michigan standards (4.1) effective use of the English language and (4.2) language variety.

Too often, skills in listening, participating in groups, speaking in small and large group settings, and problem-solving with others are overlooked as preservice students plan units of instruction. In Mrs. Smith's classroom, however, the use of standards intended to encourage these essential skills was readily apparent. Throughout the lesson observed, it was clear that students relied on one another to explore texts, think about literal and more elusive meanings, and build connections to their lived realities as well as to the realities of others. In the process, essential standards described by NCTE/IRA and the National Communication Association—standards echoed in most state-level documents—were taught. In the process, students learned critically important skills for college and workplace readiness—some that overlap the critical literacy skills already noted and others that build abilities to work with others in teams; to problem-solve in creative ways; to take ownership for one's actions, opinions, and interpretations; and more.

Outstanding English teachers such as Mrs. Smith work hard to help secondary students develop the knowledge and skills necessary to "participate as knowledgeable, reflective, creative, and critical members of a variety of literacy communities" and to be able to "use spoken, written, and visual language to accomplish their own purposes" (NCTE/IRA standards 11 and 12). Clearly, these teachers want more for their students than mastery of knowledge and skills that are testable on a state-mandated exam. They strive to help their students live literate lives by immersing them in rich literacy communities in school and encouraging them to connect school-based literacy with their lives in the world.

As my students and I conclude our discussion of this video, we reflect upon the behaviors of their own former secondary teachers. In particular, I ask them to recall a teacher who stood out for them as a champion of adolescent literacy, who drew upon strong teaching skills to support their growth as participants in our broader society, as individuals who felt empowered and comfortable drawing upon their own wide range of literacy skills to serve self-identified purposes. As we reflect, discuss, and chart specific recollections of lessons, units, teaching strategies, and teacher behaviors, I encourage preservice teachers to use their state standards as a framework for analyzing the ways masterful teachers have reflected rigor and challenge in their instructional expectations for many years.

And yet I also want my students to realize that teaching is always a process of carefully considering where we are in light of where we need or want to be. As we touch briefly on those things that we did not see in Mrs. Smith's lesson, we revisit the fact that new standards bring with them new expectations that frequently disrupt our instructional comfort zone. New expectations require change, and sometimes change is uncomfortable to consider. Unpacking the lessons and units we teach allows us to know where we are in this instructional journey, a process that reassures us that we are already doing many things right. It also allows us to look critically at those areas of instruction that need strengthening, to consider which student populations might be less well served, and to take steps toward strengthening instruction for all.

The process that my students and I experienced as we worked our way toward a mental picture of how teachers represent standards in their day-to-day instruction is similar to that which I've observed in schools across multiple states as teachers begin to align their current instruction in relation to new expectations. Along the way, the process often illuminates observations, raises questions and concerns, and opens up curriculum development work that could not have been anticipated before the alignment process was begun. Looking at two groups of teachers from distinctly different school districts may help illustrate the value and pitfalls of alignment projects.

Vignette 2: An Organic Approach to Standards Implementation and Curricular Planning

As its name suggests, University School District (USD) is located in a city heavily influenced by the sprawling university for which the town is known. Because of its location and proximity to this powerful university community, USD tends to be a district that attracts an exceptionally well-qualified cadre of teachers who are under constant public scrutiny. The student body in USD reflects radical diversity in socioeconomics and educational status as well as substantial ethnic and racial diversity. By most measures, USD has prepared students well for decades, boasting a national reputation for innovation. A substantial number of students from the district's high schools graduate and move on to universities across the country each year. Traditionally, teachers in the USD have maintained a high degree of independence in curricular planning, and most decisions about what would be taught in each of the secondary grades rested with the teachers in the individual schools.

With the introduction of the first Michigan standards in the early 1990s, individual teachers worked to align their instructional practices to the standards. However, by 2006, when the State of Michigan rolled out more stringent expectations for high schools that included revised standards for English language arts, administrators in the USD began to raise questions about the level of curricular flexibility existing in the district. Rather than offering rigidly constructed English 9, English 10, English 11, and English 12 courses, for example, the high schools boast some common required classes but also a variety of elective English classes from which students can choose subject matter that meets their needs and interests. Questions with which administrators struggled include:

- How can we be sure that students are being taught all the standards that are required at each grade level?

- How can we be sure that there are not gaps in the skills, knowledge, and content being presented?

- What is to prevent students from being taught the same pieces of literature again and again in various grade levels?

- How can we be sure that students who transfer from one school to another, or even one district or state to another, won't repeat the same materials instead of moving forward in the curriculum?

Certainly, from an administrative perspective, it would be easier to chart student progress in relation to the standards if a prescribed and mandated curriculum were in place. Yet the implications of such standardization would represent a radical departure from the ways in which teachers had been able to tailor curriculum to address student needs. The possibility of moving toward curricular standardization opened up many new questions, too. For example, wasn't it possible to address standards through myriad curricular materials? Couldn't assessments be aligned to standards but not necessarily dependent on any particular unit, novel, or author?

Though similar types of questions were being asked by administrators in other content areas as well, the questions themselves reflected some misguided assumptions about the English language arts. Absent from the questions was a recognition that literacy development is highly integrated and recursive, and that particular outcomes can be achieved by following many different paths. Though it certainly makes sense to have conversations about curricular articulation and alignment with standards, elevating those discussions beyond particular units or texts allows teachers needed flexibility to meet specific student needs and address specific student interests. As easy as it might be to think otherwise, English language arts instruction really is different from math instruction, in which concepts and skills build tightly and logically upon one another.

In their first year of deliberation about curricular alignment with the revised standards, teachers in the USD were given two options: they were offered the opportunity to adopt the "sample" units from the state Department of Education that Nadine and her host teachers had struggled with, or, if the USD teachers chose not to follow this course, to align their own units, demonstrating how those units covered the full ninety-one content expectations—in each unit! Of course it was predictable that the teachers would resist the imposition of units of study that they did not have a hand in creating. A full year of struggle ensued as teachers spent hours attempting to catalog all the various learning activities from their existing units that mapped to the standards and expectations. When I was invited to work with the group at the conclusion of that year, the frustration was palpable, and I learned how such a cataloging effort had actually prevented the teachers from having the time to create new curriculum. As Barbara noted at the end of the year, "The only thing that has been accomplished as a result of standards implementation so far is a bunch of clerical work. I don't have time to plan! I've never been more frustrated as a teacher."

As we began our discussions, I found that the USD teachers agreed on many things. They completely recognized the importance of students not repeating the same lessons and activities semester after semester. And, despite the fact that many books can profitably be read multiple times, leading to deeper understanding, they felt it very important to draw from the many wonderful literary selections that students could read and discuss. So, of course, they agreed that coordination was a good idea, and they quickly initiated discussions between grade-level instructors about the units that were already successful at each grade level.

Time set aside in the summer of 2006 provided valuable planning time away from the day-to-day work with students. Given time and support, educators shared successful units, strategies, and materials from their own classrooms. As they created charts to map out the units that were already in place, they found unanticipated consistency in both the types of units and the themes used to focus them.

Early in their planning, the USD teachers realized the wealth of possibilities they had at their fingertips if they could only capitalize on the many outstanding units their peers had already developed. One morning they decided to suspend their work for a few hours and turned their attention to the question of outcomes. Sarah posed the question first: "Okay, so let's think of it this way . . . by the end of ninth grade, what do we all agree that our students should know and be able to do within the standards?" Over the next few days, seven different areas were identified and specific, concrete outcomes were developed for each (Figure 4.2). Suddenly it no longer mattered whether the group worked from one unit or from ten. The realization that they could use these outcomes that were aligned with the standards as a metric for development of any unit liberated the entire planning process.

Of course the USD teachers still had to make some decisions about the literature that would be used at various grade levels, but even within that process they attempted to maintain a range of options. They correctly recognized that they would be better served to work with existing resources and to use available funds to broaden the range of materials available. Thinking ahead, they also recognized that their assessments would follow the outcomes—not specific pieces of literature.

Figure 4.2. USD Outcomes for English 9

By the end of ninth grade, students will demonstrate the following:

Writing

- Demonstrates the ability to work productively in peer groups
- Uses process productively in own writing
- Demonstrates ability to vary texts depending on needs of varying audiences and purposes
- Crafts a memoir
- Crafts a literary essay with textual evidence
- Writes various types of persuasive writing
- Writes for reflection
- Demonstrates basic skills to support writing as needed for selected genres

Speaking

- Demonstrates an ability to work productively in groups
- Participates in class discussions
- Develops and delivers formal speeches for varying purposes

Representing

- Creates a speech with PowerPoint
- Creates multimedia presentations to demonstrate learning
- Creates graphic representations of traditional pieces of literature

Reading

- Identifies main ideas from varying texts
- Demonstrates strategies for critically reading multiple types of texts
- Demonstrates ability to select texts independently for personal enjoyment and to fulfill specific purposes
- Applies varied reading strategies to varying types of texts (e.g., using Reading Apprenticeship, reading across the curriculum, etc.)

Listening/Viewing

- Demonstrates critical listening skills
- Listens and participates actively in groups to provide feedback

continued on next page

Figure 4.2. Continued

Literature

- Demonstrates the ability to use literary terms to facilitate conversations about and analysis of literature and informational texts
- Demonstrates the ability to see self in literature, to see beyond self in literature, and to develop a sense of social responsibility through the use of varying critical lenses
- Demonstrates the ability to read texts for varying purposes, from varying genres, and by diverse authors

Language

- Understands and uses basic constructions (e.g., sentences, paragraphs, phrases, clauses, etc.) for varying purposes, audiences, genres
- Develops a sense of word choice as a tool for developing voice
- Demonstrates an understanding of the ways language changes to support purposes for speaking and writing

They could move forward, analyzing the units that they wanted to continue using, aligning the units with the outcomes, and enhancing the units to meet the challenges the standards offered. They could invest the limited time they had for planning in productive work that applied directly to class instruction (Figure 4.3).

Later, they could go back to check each unit once again against the standards and outcomes, back-mapping to see if they had overlooked standards or expectations that logically should have been taught at the grade level. If they identified gaps, either existing units would need to be adapted or new units would need to be created to support a fully articulated standards-based program.

Figure 4.3. Organic Planning Model

Once your group has a basic understanding of the standards and expectations, then

- Think carefully and collaboratively about the competencies students at specific levels should demonstrate.
- Consider what types of knowledge, skills, and strategies students will need to demonstrate competencies.
- Decide upon the types of products that all students should be able to produce (e.g., a research project, a portfolio of creative pieces, a persuasive speech or essay or letter).
- Decide upon the types of experiences that might best support acquisition of competencies and lead to student success in creating required products.
- Plan common assessments that are aligned to standards and that address a variety of student learning needs (e.g., projects, presentations, written products, speeches, tests, and more).

When teachers are given an opportunity for close curricular analysis, the observations they make can be reinforcing and reassuring; they can also marshal a fair amount of dissonance as instructors grapple with huge questions.

- Why are we teaching these lessons in the first place?
- What are our goals for this instruction?
- Are we *really* addressing our own instructional goals—and the standards that are expected—in substantive ways, or are we just checking off expectations and moving on?

Make no mistake, this process is hard work. And it might as easily lead to decisions about what should be dropped from a particular curriculum as to what should be added. After all, rigor has far less to do with a forced march through expectations than about deep learning of knowledge and skills that can be transferred to multiple situations and with increasingly greater sophistication over time. Regardless of the decisions teachers ultimately make from these types of deliberations, they will be conscious ones that support moving forward with confidence.

Vignette 3: Mid-State Moves toward Standards-Based Teaching

The experience of Laura, a teacher I recently met, can inform us about with the kind of journey other teachers might take as they work hard to find their own voice and place within the process of standards implementation. Laura teaches secondary English at a comprehensive mid-Michigan high school. In her fourth year of high school teaching, she draws upon the experiences she has had at Mid-State High as well as those she previously acquired working as a mentor, facilitator, and bridge between students and faculty in a Latin American college study abroad program based in Central America. There, her hands-on experiences teaching and learning in Costa Rica, Nicaragua, Guatemala, and Cuba whetted her appetite for creating authentic opportunities for students to explore the unknown and to express what they know. In addition, she has benefited from interaction with outstanding English educators through multiple self-selected and carefully structured professional development experiences that included a master's program, participation in one of the state's National Writing Project sites, and a multiyear professional development grant.

Like her peers at USD, Laura and her colleagues at Mid-State High School (MSHS) believed strongly in the types of instructional units they had individually offered for each of the four levels (honors-remedial) of their students in the tracked program of their large high school. Like my students and the teachers at USD, they entered the conversation about implementation of the new Michigan high school English standards by first individually considering the units they were already teaching and then tracking how those lessons addressed the various standards and expectations posed in the newly adopted standards. This process allowed them to examine how their current lessons aligned with the new standards and expectations and to focus on how successfully those lessons addressed the varied learning needs of all their students, thus shifting their conversation rapidly to a consideration of how they might make the curriculum more effective—not just more difficult—for a wider array of learners.

One lesson they learned early on from this consideration was the difficulty involved in drawing any sort of conclusion from their work because teachers taught entirely different units, with different books *and* different outcomes. It quickly became apparent that their tenth-grade classrooms reflected a series of instructional islands. Though they shared physical proximity in the school, they had little else in common.

As these teachers considered the lack of commonly held vision for their program, they decided to begin a process of collaborative curriculum alignment using the new standards as their guide. Laura and her fellow teachers recognized that successful instruction must build from the literacy skills that students bring with them to class, and that their job was to build student investment in literacy through a range of experiences and technological supports that engaged the learners and built from the literacy practices across their lives. They also recognized the expertise in their own group, identifying and sharing ideas for increasing instructional effectiveness.

As a result of their analysis, they found it useful to review the sample units provided by the State of Michigan, and they began to investigate the possibility of developing pacing guides for themselves that would reflect the units they ultimately decided to include in their curriculum. Their vision of pacing guides, however, quickly evolved into planning guides as they came to recognize that they couldn't *pace* the instruction until they had *offered* the instruction and gained a sense of how quickly students could master the concepts included. In other words, rather than moving immediately to pacing, the teachers realized they needed to first think about how they could connect and teach the skills they already knew were vital for teen literacy development.

As the Mid-State teachers began to collaboratively build the curriculum for grade 10, they used the following model (Figure 4.4) to help them lay out these connections for unit planning. Because these pacing/planning documents were collaboratively developed, they reflected the judgment, knowledge, and expertise of the teachers who would use them. And, as a result, they also reflected the realities of the MSHS classrooms, allowing the teachers to develop materials that would address the range of needs of their own students. While all students would work toward the same rigorous outcomes, specific reading materials and writing assign-

Figure 4.4. Grade 10—Pacing (Planning) Guide

Building on English 9, English 10 is designed to expand the student's experiences in reading, writing, speaking, and listening with progressively more challenging materials and activities. While each class may vary in pace and depth, it is expected that all students will participate in the suggested activities at a pace suitable to their ability.

Scheduling	Materials Covered	HSCEs Addressed*	Activities	Assessments

*High School Content Expectations

ments could be adjusted within agreed-upon areas of focus and levels of difficulty to better suit the interests and needs of various individuals or groups.

The academic year at Mid-State is divided into trimesters, a relatively new structure for the school and one selected to offer more options and opportunities for students. Teachers decided to plan for up to two units each trimester, leaving time for reinforcement of particular concepts, skills, and strategies as needed. In a typical six-week unit, students would experience a variety of literary genres and writing assignments, as appropriate for the unit and the students' needs.

As an example, one of the units developed a six-week instructional period on the topic of heroes, a focus for which many instructional materials exist in both anthologies and sample units (Figure 4.5). The Mid-State teachers used a combination of their own materials and drew from available resources as they chose. In this study, students would experience novels (whole and abridged texts), short stories, novel excerpts, poetry, news articles, clips from television news programs, a documentary, and more. The literature would allow for a choice of titles depending upon appropriateness for the students, and the lessons reflected the integrated and recursive nature of the English language arts. The variety of literature they included drew from both the collection in the school, allowing for the use of existing anthologies, as well as trade books selected and purchased to support the new unit.

Figure 4.5. Heroes Planning Guide/Text Possibilities

Novels	**Short Stories**
Fahrenheit 451 (with abridged CDs)	"The Sword and the Stone"
Warriors Don't Cry (novel excerpt)	"The Tale of Sir Lancelot"
The Kite Runner or *A Thousand Splendid Suns*	"The Hero"
Poems	**Media**
"The Hero"	*Star Wars* (film)
"A Wreath for Emmett Till"	*Glory* (movie clips)
"Mother to Son"	*Beyond Rangoon* (movie clips)
"Ex-Basketball Player"	Kent State Massacre (news article)
	Operation Homecoming (television news program)
	The Murder of Emmett Till (documentary clips)
	Tiananmen Square (article, pictures, lyrics)

For the heroes unit, the teachers decided to focus student writing development on persuasive writing, but the unit also included reflection journals, an analytical essay, and writing to support a group project—all building upon or using writing skills taught earlier. In addition, a wide variety of reading and writing skills and strategies were taught at appropriate, teachable moments as instructors created short mini-lessons to emphasize skills, such as word choice, use of particular types of sentence structure or punctuation, and issues of author's craft as they were evidenced in the literature being studied. Because the unit focused so heavily on *real* reading, writing, speaking, and listening tasks, it supports assessments that require students to demonstrate what they have learned by producing products, engaging in performances or discussions, and applying learning to provide a service or solve a problem.

Using the pacing/planning guide (Figure 4.4), the tenth-grade teachers aligned each of the activities with the new standards and expectations, producing some helpful observations about the types of standards and expectations that were included in the unit, and about what was not addressed. Recall that the state standards in Michigan were organized into four strands:

- Strand One: Writing, Speaking, and Expressing
- Strand Two: Reading, Listening, and Viewing
- Strand Three: Literature and Culture
- Strand Four: Language

As they viewed the charts they had developed (see the appendix), the teachers recognized that Strands One, Two, and Three are heavily stressed in this unit. They could see that students are exploring writing in many different ways—using journals to think about the literature they are reading, planning group discussions and presentations, taking a stand on an issue, and moving that into an analytical essay drawing upon all phases of a process approach to writing. Through this work, these students experience writing for many different purposes, audiences, and in varying genres, and they learn new strategies and skills as their teachers carefully select the best and most meaningful time to present or reinforce a particular concept. Reading skills are learned within the context of authentic reading experiences, and opportunities to develop as speakers, listeners, and writers are finely woven around the reading, viewing, and other experiences that thread through the unit.

In this unit, students also engage many different types of reading experiences, including fiction, nonfiction, and technical/nonfiction texts. And in so doing, they see how an author makes conscious decisions about which genre will best communicate her message for particular purposes and which conventions, sentence structures, and word choices will best support her purposes.

Because it offered them a bird's-eye view of the instructional choices being made, the type of analysis in which these teachers engaged provides a powerful tool for curricular planning. In their grade-level departmental groups, they discussed their findings and used their observations to strengthen this, and other, units. Seldom do educators have the time and support to reflect on their day-to-day teaching. The hectic pace of the school day, during which teachers work continuously with 120–160 students each day, offers little time for analysis and planning of this type. As teachers step back from their classrooms, look at the work that has taken place, and analyze their observations, they can often make more conscious instructional decisions.

In this particular case, teachers were pleased with the literary choices they had made and the types of writing students would experience. Reading and writing skills instruction would build upon work already mapped out for ninth grade and would allow many opportunities for short lessons (mini-lessons): the skills and strategies presented could be moved immediately into use by the students, providing practical and effective reinforcement. However, the pacing/planning guide also revealed that the study of language would be largely absent from this unit, though of course there are many junctures where attention could be drawn to the use of dialects, formal versus informal uses of language, sentence structure, and more.

By observing the lack of emphasis on language study, teachers were able to collaborate on ways to enhance student awareness of essential language features. For example, in relation to passages being discussed, attention could be drawn to why authors vary their sentence lengths and structures; how authors manipulate their readers through word choice, vernacular, use of fragments, use of metaphors, and more; and when and why an author would choose to break the rules.

Because Laura and her colleagues were so actively involved in planning their own ninth- and tenth-grade program, they were able to build in skills and strategy

lessons that they felt were important for their students. The process of collaborative planning in which they engaged allowed them to draw from individual teacher
expertise, borrow ideas from each other, and tailor tried-and-true plans to better
meet new challenges. They could build from the literature they had available in
their own bookroom, too, and then enhance this with new literature, including
literary nonfiction and technical texts.

Still, despite all this work, a full year into the process of curricular alignment,
Laura and her colleagues found that their questions and concerns had shifted.
Though many of their units were in implementation phases, they found themselves
revisiting and questioning some of their fundamental goals for instruction. As
Laura noted,

> The units are better for sure, but the emphasis is still on the books! I'm still all about
> novel studies when what I really want to be about is big ideas, big questions. I'm not
> sure my students are getting a glimmer of the real reason we are focusing on "Heroes"
> or "The Courage to Find Oneself" or "Choices: We Must Take Sides." Somehow
> I need to shift things to capture the focus so that students can see how all this really
> relates to them instead of just bogging them down with details!

A glimpse back at the planning guide used to create the units helps to explain
what had occurred. Though a helpful tool in supporting the teachers in their early
conversations about curricular consistency and standards alignment, the guides
encouraged teachers to focus almost exclusively on materials, content expectations,
activities, and assessments. The guides provided no support or encouragement to
take the next critical step that Laura now desired, a step that would require her to
consider one of the most fundamental instructional questions of all: *why am I doing
this?* With this question, Laura pushed herself to consider her rationale for every
instructional decision she made in her classroom.

Exploring this question helped her realize that she must interrogate not only
the larger goals for the units she taught, but also the activities that she provided her
students each and every day to meet those goals. For example, if she seeks to develop within her students a love of literature as a source of pleasure and recreation,
the activities in her classroom must support that goal. The precious moments
that she shares with her students should not be squandered on worksheets, word
finds, book reports, or any other time-consuming activities unless she is confident
that such work will lead to the goals and outcomes she has set. Not only must her
activities in class support her goals, but also the assessments she chooses must be
consistent with them.

In short, shifting the focus to big-picture goals and planning from that point,
selecting materials and activities and assessments to meet those instructional goals,
allows every action in the classroom to align in a highly strategic way. The process

sounds simple, but anyone who has ever taught can attest to how radically this type of planning departs from the status quo of schooling. Consider how textbooks and adopted booklists are often selected in complete isolation from the daily work of the classroom, particularly in state adoptions that place these decisions beyond even the school district level. When this happens, instructional focus too often shifts to covering particular materials instead of understanding particular concepts or exploring particular questions. Think of how much more fragmented the instructional vision for the classroom might be if teachers are also mandated to use units of instruction for which they have little ownership, and likely no sense of the global ideas the units are intended to represent?

Aligning Goals with Standards

When I work with students like Nadine who create multiweek units in my methods classroom, I start by asking them to think about this question: *why am I doing this?* I want them to think early and to think hard about the literacy goals they want their students to achieve. As their goals take on focus, we revisit the standards that they are responsible for and consider together how they might be addressed. Once we have these goals and standards in mind, we consider questions that are rich and interesting enough to warrant a study that might account for weeks of valuable instructional time. If we, as teachers, are not intrigued by the questions, how can we possibly expect our students to be? And if students and teachers are not engaged in this way, how can there be any hope of avoiding a sense of dissociation from the important ideas of the discipline that make literacy essential for our students?

Only after we have carefully considered the goals and essential questions for a particular unit of study do we consider the books and activities and assessments that will go into the daily plans. It is a model that feels foreign at first, particularly to teachers—new and veteran—who have been forced to plan curriculum based on the availability of books that have been in the storage room for years or from a checklist of skills to be covered. Yet once students have familiarity with this model as a planning tool, they are able to see how each part of the unit flows naturally from the outcomes they should achieve.

Using one of the heroes units that the Mid-State teachers planned for the first trimester as an example, we can observe how this planning process might unfold. Starting with some focus questions for such a unit on heroes, teachers might want adolescents to consider:

- What does it mean to be a hero now? In the past?
- What qualities do heroes exemplify?
- How and where do we see acts of heroism in the world around us?

- What qualities do they themselves possess that might help them become a hero for someone in their lives?

With these questions in mind, specific literacy goals can be established that align with the Michigan standards. Again, as examples, teachers might choose to orient their units around goals such as these:

- Students will read, discuss, and appreciate a rich variety of texts as they consider heroes past and present and link their understanding to their own lives.

- Students will listen to accounts of heroism from a variety of media sources and participate in discussions through which they can come to understand the many dimensions of heroism in the world around them.

- Students will engage in many different types of writing, exploring a biographical sketch in depth as they examine acts of heroism in their community.

And to support these goals for student learning, we might find the following qualities that reflect the best of what we know about adolescent literacy:

- Teachers would select engaging materials from among those identified for the unit. These materials represent a wide range of sources, reflecting varying perspectives as well as varying visions of heroism across the centuries. Young adult fiction and poetry as well as classic literary fiction and nonfiction, articles from contemporary newspapers and magazines, films, and more might find their way into the classroom.

- Students would be invited to bring in materials from home, and certainly they would be encouraged to think about the focus questions for the unit from the vantage point of each student's own life, family, and culture.

- The types of writing that are assigned during the study would encourage student thinking about the information at hand, and some assignments would likely be tailored to enrich student understanding of a particular genre.

- This unit would provide logical connections to many genres through which discussions about language use, writer's style, and more could be highlighted. Assessments would follow logically from the major goals for the unit, focusing on final products that could include presentations, performances, final draft papers or projects, or more.

This is a process marked by continuous growth for the teachers involved because it requires a teacher-researcher stance. Day-to-day planning becomes an invitation to professional growth as each step in the planning process leads to new—and often more challenging—questions (Figure 4.6). Certainly the work of the teachers highlighted here will support changes in classroom instruction. And in clear contrast to the frustration, anger, and resignation of educators with whom Nadine worked, discussed at the beginning of this chapter, the teacher-empowered planning also resulted in changes in the professional investment and ownership of teachers, a process best accomplished with sustained support.

Figure 4.6. What Do These Stories Tell Us?

- Start with examples of excellent instruction, whether that includes viewing a video, visiting the classroom of a peer, or both. Take good notes and then take time to reflect on what you saw. What do you observe that you consider excellent literacy instruction? How do these elements of excellent instruction relate to your own teaching? To the ways excellent teachers in your background taught?

- Unpack your observations with others. What types of practices did all of you notice? How did the lesson you observed reflect the standards that are being implemented? What standards were included? Which ones weren't addressed? What suggestions could you make for enhancing the lesson?

- Look at a unit that you enjoy teaching. Using the new standards for literacy as a filter, what are you doing well already? For whom is the current instruction working best? Is anyone left out? If so, is there any way to adjust instruction so that more students can be successful?

- What new questions do you have at this point in your planning? Share your question or questions with colleagues. Consider selecting one or more as a focus for instructional planning for next year.

In Part 3, I look at ways that teachers can become more involved in shaping the course of adolescent literacy in a standards-based model. Before that, it is important to think about one other critical variable affecting standards and their implementation. Like a thousand-pound invisible elephant in the room, testing—and the broader consideration of assessment—has had an enormous impact on instruction. Probably all teachers have felt the effect of testing on their students. However, it's not enough to feel that something is wrong: we have to understand what's happening and then do something about it. In Chapter 5, we look specifically at how testing may be working against our best efforts to promote adolescent literacy.

Chapter Five

Do We Value What We Test? Do We Test What We Value?

So what's the connection? My principal told us that we have to get the kids ready for the Merit Exams . . . but that's just the ACT and a timed writing sample. What's that got to do with higher standards?
(Michigan teacher, 2008)

Sarah's frustration is understandable. As standards have grown in sophistication and breadth, the measures of achievement associated with instruction have clearly failed to keep pace. Standards that are intended to raise the achievement bar for all students are still assessed by examinations that are timed, largely multiple choice, and narrow in focus. As a result, they not only favor particular types of students, but they also favor particular parts of the curriculum, placing great weight on some standards and completely ignoring others. To make matters worse, the students who do poorly on the types of assessments typically used are often quite capable of demonstrating their learning in other ways, and the skills that are ignored on high-stakes exams are frequently as critical—and in many cases far more critical—than those that find their way onto the assessments.

In the fall of 2008, both presidential candidates described plans to address the crisis of failing schools. Neither, however, paused to explain how those failures are determined, what measures are used as evidence of school failure, nor how credible the assessments or the data they provide might be. In a sense, both candidates fell victim to the use of highly suspect data that purport to measure particular levels of achievement on essential academic knowledge and skills, and in the heat of a campaign, offered up remarkably simplistic solutions for very complicated situations.

Assessment—most often recognized in the popular press as testing—has become integrally ingrained in the national effort to raise student achievement at all levels. Testing has become the tool that allows politicians and policymakers to issue sweeping judgments that label many students—along with their teachers and schools—as *FAILING* and with little opportunity to interrogate the label or the reasons for it. One thing we know for sure: each and every assessment created and put before adolescents on a regular basis reflects values. In the wake of No Child Left Behind, rising dropout rates, and a continued adolescent literacy crisis, perhaps it is time to take a step back and reconsider the values these assessments represent.

If we stop for a moment to analyze the assessment frenzy, we quickly see that the nature of the assessments themselves tells us a great deal. Though national and state standards often describe a rich array of literacy experiences intended to support students as they develop an appreciation for reading classic and contemporary texts that they will use as a basis to understand their own lives and those of others, the tests used to measure student mastery of grade-level expectations generally find these goals far too difficult to assess, and instead focus on discrete and testable comprehension and vocabulary skills. Standards typically include expectations that students will learn many writing and speaking skills that will equip them to draw upon their own sense of process as they write and speak for many different purposes and audiences, yet both end-of-grade and high school exit tests typically omit speaking and listening altogether, and writing is often assessed in the most reductive way possible—with multiple-choice punctuation and usage questions and with one or more timed writing assessment that separates student writers from the tools they have been taught and urged to use in real life written communication. Good standards place significant value on understanding the power of language as students navigate styles, dialects, and conventions to craft and to understand messages. Tests place sole value on correct use of accepted conventions without accommodation for the fact that real writers and speakers frequently draw upon nonstandard language use to make a point or create a perspective most effectively.

Standards suggest literacy instruction that is broad-based, that responds to individual needs and contexts, and that offers a basis for full participation in citizenship. And yet we find ourselves at a juncture where many educators have been forced to acknowledge that "actions speak louder than words." Despite what legislators and policymakers have said through the adoption of rigorous standards, the reality is that the things that are tested are the things that must be taught, particularly when tests are used to make judgments about students and their schools. Sadly, much of the good work that has been accomplished in articulating higher standards and bringing those standards into the classroom is at risk of being derailed by the very tests that are used to assess student progress.

If we examine the tests—and I think we must—we have no choice but to ask, *are we really testing what we value?* The disjuncture between most state standards and the tests that have been put in place to assess student progress continue to elicit confusion and frustration from teachers. For example, in a recent workshop I asked teachers from two schools to identify the most important things they teach in their secondary English language arts classes. Predictable answers came from around the room: literature—both young adult and classic; authentic writing experiences that provide a platform for teaching strategies and skills; interactive projects that support hands-on experiences with research, technologically supported presentations, and service learning—these, and more, were the things teachers identified as essential for their students' literacy development. I quickly recorded the teacher responses in a large circle that ultimately became part of a Venn diagram. In a second circle, the teachers and I collaboratively listed the areas of the discipline that were actually assessed on the state exit exam. Finally, we overlapped the two circles, examining closely those aspects of the total curriculum that were actually focused upon on the test. The comparison was stark: a mere fraction of what was valued—both in the state standards and by the teachers themselves—was actually included in the assessments.

Certainly, tests can only provide representative data on student achievement, but for teachers and administrators who risk having their students and their programs labeled as failing based on the results of a test, the types of knowledge and skills on high-stakes assessments take on incredible significance. In some cases, the pressure to help students pass the test leads to curricular decisions that privilege certain literacy skills over others; for example, because questions about the correct use of the semicolon are on the test, valuable class time must be used to teach and practice semicolon rules and usage, too often in out-of-context exercises. Unfortunately, since making personal connections to great literature—and even reading for pleasure—are typically not testable, these literacy goals may be squeezed out of the instructional day as time to focus on commas, semicolons, and the correct use of *whom/who* is carved out.

Tests reveal other things, too. They tell us a great deal about the types of intelligences—and the types of students—that are valued. Almost any parent of two or more children can attest to the fact that adolescents are not all the same. They have different talents, interests, and skills. Some are far more proficient in demonstrating their achievement through a paper-and-pen test than their peers. Think of the concern that might be raised if all students were required to demonstrate knowledge through a performance or through the creation of an artistic work? How much more concern would be heard if this were the only way to demonstrate knowledge on an exit test that might have real impact on successful high school or end-of-grade completion? For so many adolescents who struggle with timed, written, nonauthentic tests, discrimination is pervasive in the types of assessments they are forced to take year after year. If we value *all* of the students, surely multiple measures reflecting different types of assessment are in order, particularly for high-stakes decision making.

Interestingly, assessments likely reveal more about the assessors than they do about the students who take the tests. As one analyzes the pervasive presence of decontextualized content and skills-based questions that provide, at best, snippets of information removed from the context of authentic language and literacy use, a misguided set of foundational assumptions about literacy is revealed. Instead of literacy that creates power with language and texts, value is placed on a checklist of culturally accepted correct answers. Digging deeper, the fact that tests place such value on these items suggests that teens who come from less traditional, mainstream backgrounds should spend the precious moments of instructional time concentrating on such secondary and minute skills instead of engaging in a rich exploration of literature and social engagement in speaking, listening, and writing that helps them establish and develop their voices in the world. What could possibly motivate this type of action? At the very least, before we unleash high-stakes testing on our children, we should ask that question.

Though it's easy to see why tests might focus on the items they do, unfortunately, they also work at cross purposes with our high expectations for twenty-first-century literacy. Unless we are careful, the very best work of the past several decades intended to promote twenty-first-century literacies will be lost, and a generation of young adults will enter college, the workplace, and life with inadequate literacy skills. Simply put, when it comes to high-stakes testing, educators, parents and policymakers have no choice but to pay a great deal more attention than ever before to the values—both in terms of who and what is valued—in high-stakes tests that are used to make judgments about adolescents and their schools.

When Do Assessments Help?

Certainly, assessments can be extraordinarily helpful to instruction. As classroom teachers, we use both formative and summative assessment regularly to gauge student achievement and modify instructional delivery in response to student needs.

Every time a teacher begins a class with a short "fast-write" assignment in response to a prompt based on previous learning, students are given a moment to connect to previous lessons, reconnect to homework that might have been completed the night before, and prepare for the learning at hand. These very brief assessments also offer valuable information to the teacher, helping him or her to see quickly where connections (and misconnections) have been made. The information a professional teacher learns from formative assessments will likely determine the point of entry into the day's lesson or the need for a new strategy or technique to help clarify an important concept or answer a question. If students have not learned essential concepts from the previous day, then that becomes the place to start.

Formative assessments help students as well. They provide a time to stop and focus, to reflect, and to raise questions. The lives of adolescents are remarkably busy, making it essential to create spaces where new knowledge, skills, and processes can be contextualized in meaningful ways. Formative assessments (Figure 5.1) help to provide these opportunities; they can be written—fast-writes, entrance-and-exit slips, two-minute responses, learning logs, reflection notes, and more—or they can draw upon the highly social nature of adolescents as students share reflections in small groups; offer brainstormed responses to a prompt; engage in a quick think-pair-share in which two or more students think about a prompt together, share their individual ideas, and then share their collaborative ideas with the large group; and more. Because of the integral place formative assessments hold in instruction, they become critical tools for teachers and for students as they wend their way through complex ideas emerging from integrated literary study.

Summative assessments (Figure 5.2) that remain deeply rooted in the classroom are helpful in many ways, too. Though sometimes these assessments do take the form of tests, they frequently extend to much more authentic expressions of learning that require students to move beyond memorizing, summarizing, and interpreting, and on to analyzing, synthesizing, and evaluating (Bloom). For example, in my own classes we read and discuss characters and events from *To Kill*

Figure 5.1. Helpful Formative Assessments

- fast writes
- entrance slips
- exit slips
- two-minute responses
- learning logs
- reflection notes
- think-pair-share moments

Figure 5.2. Helpful Summative Assessments

- thoughtful and contextualized tests
- performances
- debates
- mock trials
- development of papers, newspapers, webpages, blogs, hypermedia
- demonstrations
- applications that extend reading comprehension and analysis

---

a Mockingbird by Harper Lee. The book opens up many topics of discussion that are highly complex and compelling for today's citizens. As one of the assessments at the end of the unit of study, I ask students to select a character unlike themselves (perhaps of a different gender, age, or race than themselves), to select one of the theoretical perspectives we have been studying, and to use that perspective to create a monologue in the voice of the character that is rooted in, but extends beyond, the text. The creation and presentation of these five-minute monologues prove to be challenging tasks because they require the students to build from knowledge to higher levels of thinking. Because students perform their monologues for their peers, the assessment allows students and me to think about their progress on a broad spectrum of essential literacy skills.

Carefully developed summative assessments help teachers adjust and tailor instruction. Before instructional units are begun, teachers in the Mid-State School District and elsewhere across Michigan and the nation consider the outcomes students will meet as a result of instruction. Once outcomes are determined in conjunction with the standards and other curricular requirements of a particular locale, assessments can be considered. By thinking of these things first, instruction can be tailored carefully through daily plans that support differentiation of instruction as needed to meet the outcomes and prepare for assessments. Final assessments may include a menu of options—including performances, presentations, debates, mock trails, papers, newspapers, webpages, blogs, or hypermedia, and more—thus allowing for differentiation of the assessments so that all students experience a range of ways to demonstrate literacy growth.

From Classroom-Based to District-Based Assessments

When assessments are closely aligned with the day-to-day work of the classroom, they fulfill a variety of instructional purposes. As assessments move further from the classroom, their purposes change and the correlation to the full spectrum of content included in the classroom is reduced. Whereas classroom-based assessment is intended to measure individual student performance with an eye toward instructional change, standard end-of-grade and high school exit tests are developed to allow districts to compare the performance of groups of students on specific types of items. These comparisons, taken as representations of the types of learning success in the school, are used to draw sweeping conclusions about students, teachers, schools, and even entire school districts. As described earlier, this can be a dangerous situation in light of multiple factors—primarily that such tests favor certain groups of students, types of learners, and parts of the curriculum.

The temptation to put faith in standardized tests is very powerful, though. Legislators want a means of determining which schools are performing according to particular expectations. Parents moving into new communities want an index of successful schools to help narrow their search for the best neighborhoods and schools for their children. The media demand some sort of comparison that can be used to make judgments about schools and districts. Because the temptation to create and trust such measures of achievement is so strong, it becomes critical that educators take an active role in helping shape those assessments and in helping the public understand what the data generated from them actually mean.

In the State of Michigan, the members of the committee that revised the state's high school literacy standards were determined to avoid end-of-grade standardized tests for the reasons described earlier. Instead, the committee argued that the most authentic end-of-grade assessments would be those that districts developed in response to the standards-based instruction in the schools. The thinking behind that decision was straightforward: if teachers in each district agreed upon the outcomes and created instructional units for each grade level, they could create assessments of the outcomes that would, in turn, provide comparative data for the state. The data would be more meaningful because they would reflect a broader base of the state standards than traditional, timed exams could provide.

Teachers in the University School District (USD) embraced the challenge of creating their own end-of-grade assessment in the summer of 2007 (Figure 5.3). A large group of teachers from ninth grade met for a week to discuss the advantages of various types of assessments, and they ultimately decided to implement an end-of-grade portfolio that could be assessed with a standard rubric that all the teachers could agree upon. The portfolio would include authentic pieces of student writing that grew from process-writing assignments that actually demonstrated what students knew and could do when they had access to all the tools the teachers were expecting them to learn about and use in the classroom.

Unfortunately, portfolios are not familiar to all teachers, and sometimes district leaders have difficulty seeing how they can provide the comparative, objective data that states require. The belief that portfolios cannot provide the same level of

Figure 5.3. English Common Assessment Part I

A portfolio is a collection of your work from this class that will:

1. Document your growth as a reader and writer, speaker and listener.
2. Demonstrate your ability to reflect on your learning in English.
3. Demonstrate your mastery of the content we've studied during this class.

PART I: Reflective Writing Overview
As a guide through your portfolio, you will respond to four reflective prompts that will require you to use evidence from exercises and assignments from this class to demonstrate your thinking and practice. Discuss specific evidence from your work in this class. When you are finished, you will have four separate reflective pieces tied to the Michigan High School Content Expectations for English Language Arts. Your class will determine the appropriate length and development of the four reflections. The English Common Assessment will be used for all English classes at the high school level.

A. Writing, Speaking, and Expressing
For this section you are expected to write thoughtfully about how you express yourself in writing, speaking, and other modes of presentation and expression. As you discuss your development and creative process (how you plan, prepare, and present your ideas), reference specific examples from your work and experience to support your statements. For example, you may use excerpts from narratives, essays, speeches, theatrical presentations, audio/visual presentations, etc., that you have created in this class to support your claims.

B. Reading, Listening, and Viewing
For this section you are expected to write thoughtfully about the strategies you use to understand and interpret what you read, hear, and see. As you discuss your development and reading/interpretive process, reference specific examples from your work and experience in this class to support your statements. For example, you may use excerpts from writing about literature, essays, reader response letters, double-entry journals, and other reading, listening, and viewing strategies.

C. Literature and Culture
For this section you are expected to write thoughtfully about your understanding of the historical, literary, and cultural content of the course. Literature is defined broadly to include classic and contemporary fiction, poetry, nonfiction, mass media, film, and other texts from popular culture. As you discuss your understanding of literature and texts, using the terminology of literature including literary devices and movements, consider making text-to-text, text-to-self, and text-to-world connections.

D. Language
For this section you are expected to demonstrate your awareness of the technical and mechanical aspects of writing in a variety of contexts and settings as a reader and writer. For example, you may use excerpts from rough and final drafts and/or peer conferencing to support examples of your growth as a writer and editor in this class with regard to sentence structure, word choice, punctuation, etc.

objectivity as multiple-choice tests reflects, of course, many layers of assumptions. Perhaps the most noteworthy is the assumption that traditional tests are objective. Certainly, they do offer the option of correct or incorrect answers. Beyond that, however, they provide a narrow snapshot of literacy that assumes the questions represent the most important information students should have learned in particular educational settings and that the questions and format are equally fair for all learners. As described earlier, these assumptions are often incorrect.

The teachers in USD designed their grade-level portfolio to be aligned closely with state standards in specific and visible ways and manageable and appropriate for various grade levels in the diverse secondary schools in the district. Furthermore, it was designed to promote higher levels of student thinking and demonstrations of learning in the most authentic manner possible for generating comparative data.

To provide for comparative data, the assessment committee designed a rubric (Figure 5.4) that, following training, all teachers across the district regardless of their program could use to provide data that would describe student progress. The rubric, in the same manner as the portfolio, was designed to directly reflect the various stands and standards adopted by the state.

Despite the close alignment to the standards, district administrators and some teachers retained concerns about portfolios as a district-level assessment tool. Despite the authenticity of the tool, concerns focused on the potential subjectivity of the process. Questions were raised about the ways teachers would use the portfolio assignment and the rubric. Would the portfolio really prove to be a reliable tool? Would the results offer inner-rater reliability? Proponents of the portfolio recognized the direct ways that assessment drives instruction. They also knew that portfolios offer a much more authentic and fair means of assessment for many of their students, so they argued for a compromise to protect the portfolio portion of the assessment program. Ultimately, they agreed to adding two other measures to the end-of-grade assessment: a standard test of reading comprehension and student writing samples scored by MY Access, a computerized system for providing response to student work.

The MY Access program offers an alluring prospect for teachers of English language arts who are often buried under the burden of student papers needing teacher response. MY Access offers students quick comments back on word choice, sentence structure, and other writing basics and purports to be aligned with the 6+1 Trait assessment rubric. However, even such a promising prospect offers a downside. To score papers, MY Access has to be programmed. That means that someone must build into the system algorithms that score for sentence structure, word choice, and logical development. For the system to work, predictability for each of these must be anticipated in advance for particular types of writing. Once again, questions emerge regarding the compatibility of such practice and assessment with the intent of the standards that address the necessity of providing all students with the opportunity to develop skill in writing for a wide variety of rhetorical purposes and drawing upon appropriate tools for varying audiences and genres. If only predictable and preprogrammed responses are possible, how will

Figure 5.4. PART I: Reflective Writing Rubric

	4	3	2	1	0
A. Writing, Speaking, and Expressing					
Writing quality	Clearly focused and purposefully organized; unique to the student's experience as a writer, speaker, and presenter.	Generally well-organized and focused on the student's individual experience as a writer, speaker, and presenter.	Writing sometimes loses focus and/or is loosely organized; examples are general as a writer, speaker, and presenter.	Poorly focused and organized without specific examples as a writer, speaker, and presenter.	No focus and without specific examples as a writer, speaker and presenter.
Reflective	Deeply analytical, insightful discussion of student's growth as a writer, speaker, and presenter.	Generally analytical and insightful discussion of student's growth.	Somewhat insightful and observant discussion of student's growth.	Observations of growth are inaccurate and/or not justified with evidence.	No discussion of student growth.
Literary context	Demonstrates thorough and subtle understanding of writing process in both individual and group settings.	Demonstrates comprehensive understanding of the writing process in both individual and group settings.	Demonstrates general understanding of writing process in both individual and group settings.	General knowledge of the writing process is unsupported by evidence.	Little to no awareness of the writing process.
Mechanics and conventions	Fluent control of word choice, grammar, and punctuation with very few errors.	Adequate control of word choice, grammar, and punctuation with predictable errors.	General control of word choice, grammar, and punctuation with occasional errors.	Poor control of word choice, grammar, and punctuation with many errors, but message is intact.	Little mechanical control with numerous errors that distract from message.
B. Reading, Listening, and Viewing					
Writing quality	Clearly focused and purposefully organized; unique to the student's experience as a reader and audience.	Generally well-organized and focused on the student's individual experience as a reader and audience.	Writing sometimes loses focus and/or is loosely organized; examples are general as a reader and audience.	Poorly focused and organized without specific examples as a reader and audience.	No focus and without specific examples as a reader and audience.
Reflective	Deeply analytical, insightful discussion of student's improved awareness as a reader and audience.	Generally analytical and insightful discussion of student's growth as reader and audience.	Somewhat insightful and observant discussion of student's growth as reader and audience.	Observations of growth are inaccurate and/or not justified with evidence.	No discussion of student growth.
Literary context	Demonstrates thorough and subtle understanding of author's craft and the role of the reader.	Demonstrates comprehensive understanding of the author's craft.	Demonstrates general understanding of author's craft.	General knowledge of the author's craft is unsupported by evidence.	Little to no awareness of the author's craft.
Mechanics and conventions	Fluent control of word choice, grammar, and punctuation with very few errors.	Adequate control of word choice, grammar, and punctuation with predictable errors.	General control of word choice, grammar, and punctuation with occasional errors.	Poor control of word choice, grammar, and punctuation with many errors, but message is intact.	Little mechanical control with numerous errors that distract from message.

continued on next page

C. Literature and Culture				
Writing quality	Clearly focused and purposefully organized; unique to individual experience and understanding of course content.	Generally well-organized and focused on the individual experience and understanding of course content.	Writing sometimes loses focus and/or is loosely organized; general awareness of course content.	Poorly focused and organized without specific examples from the course.	No focus and without specific examples.
Reflective	Deeply analytical, insightful discussion of cultural, historical, and literary issues raised through the course.	Generally insightful discussion of cultural, historical, and literary issues raised through the course.	Somewhat observant discussion of cultural, historical, and literary issues raised through the course.	Observations of course content are inaccurate and/or not adequately explored.	No discussion of content.
Literary context	Demonstrates thorough understanding and use of literary, historical, and cultural terms.	Demonstrates comprehensive understanding and use of literary, historical, and cultural terms.	Demonstrates general understanding and use of literary, historical, and cultural terms.	Use of terms is largely inaccurate.	Little to no awareness of literary, historical, and cultural terms.
Mechanics and conventions	Fluent control of word choice, grammar, and punctuation with very few errors.	Adequate control of word choice, grammar, and punctuation with predictable errors.	General control of word choice, grammar, and punctuation with occasional errors.	Poor control of word choice, grammar, and punctuation with many errors, but message is intact.	Little mechanical control with numerous errors that distract from message.
D. Language				
Writing quality	Clearly focused and purposefully organized; unique to the student's experience as a writer, reader, and editor.	Generally well-organized and focused on the student's experience as a writer, reader, and editor.	Writing sometimes loses focus and/or is loosely organized; examples are general.	Poorly focused and organized without specific examples from writing, reading, and editing.	No focus and without specific examples.
Reflective	Insightful discussion of student's growth as a writer, speaker, and editor.	Generally insightful discussion of student's growth as a writer, speaker, and editor.	Somewhat insightful and observant discussion of student's growth.	Observations of growth are inaccurate and/or not justified with evidence.	No discussion of student growth.
Literary context	Demonstrates thorough and subtle understanding of word choice, grammar, and mechanics.	Demonstrates comprehensive understanding of word choice, grammar, and mechanics.	Demonstrates general understanding of word choice, grammar, and mechanics.	General knowledge of the word choice, grammar, and mechanics is unsupported by evidence.	Little to no awareness of the technical aspects of language.
Mechanics and conventions	Fluent control of word choice, grammar, and punctuation with very few errors.	Adequate control of word choice, grammar, and punctuation with predictable errors.	General control of word choice, grammar, and punctuation with occasional errors.	Poor control of word choice, grammar, punctuation with many errors, but message is intact.	Little mechanical control with numerous errors that distract from message.

creativity fare? Would William Shakespeare, Samuel Clemens, or Chris Crutcher be considered proficient as a writer?

None of this is to say there is no place for technologically supported responses to student writing. It is, however, a caution. If the message back to the classroom by any assessment or any tool, purchased program, or methodology is that only one type of writing is valued, decision makers should be 100 percent sure that is the message they want to convey. If passing a high-stakes test is dependent upon formulaic writing, schools will—and many currently do—invest significant instructional and professional development time on this type of writing. Educational communities and policymakers alike must be very sure about what the assessments they impose actually encourage. They will likely get what they ask for.

Assessment beyond the District and School

Assessments designed to generate comparative data have been a part of state assessments for decades. In many states, original work on state-level literacy assessments attempted to survey as wide a base of literacy skills as possible. In many cases, tools for evaluating oral language, listening, and literary appreciation were included in annual assessments. Unfortunately, broad-based use of such tools proved to be both time-consuming and expensive, initiating efforts to create assessments that are more efficient and resulting in the development of snapshot assessments intended to demonstrate representative findings for groups of students.

Exit tests have become increasingly high stakes for students over the past two decades. In Michigan, the State Board had listened to Achieve, Inc., when that body advocated for an exit test that would be nationally recognized by universities and colleges, as well as to the state principals who wanted a more efficient assessment system. In large part in response to these groups, policymakers at the state level adopted the ACT as the core for the state literacy exit test, to be supplemented by a timed essay writing assessment. As a result of the decision to implement this plan, every high school student in the state takes the ACT and the supplemental parts of the statewide Merit Exam. The problem? The ACT is a nationally normed test designed to predict first-year college success. It was not developed or modified to reflect the state standards of Michigan. The multiple-choice format of the ACT focuses on skills of comprehension, interpretation, and analysis, and addresses specific writing skills—all tested in a multiple-choice format. Certainly, all of these skills are subsumed within the Michigan standards, but not in the decontextualized fashion reflected in the test. Because of the significance placed on test scores by individuals and groups who use them to make judgments about students, schools, and districts, the impact of the test has potentially extraordinarily negative consequences for curricular reform and, hence, adolescent literacy.

Despite the tremendous impact of testing on curriculum and on the day-to-day instruction in the classroom, it is likely that the full import of assessments on adolescent literacy has been underestimated. Without serious examination into the ways high-stakes end-of-grade and exit tests affect the full implementation and realization of standards in every state, it is possible—indeed, it is likely—that the intent and the very noble goals of the standards movement will be derailed by the very assessments chosen to judge the success of their implementation.

3 Claiming Agency— Reaching In and Reaching Out

Over the past several decades, educational reform has become firmly rooted in American media, policy, and legislation. In many cases, the movement toward standards has been well intended, and in cases where sufficient teacher and administrator involvement have been included, the actual standards have provided excellent models that map particular disciplines and raise important questions about equity, access, and appropriateness for students as well as questions about time, resources, and support for teachers.

In too many cases, however, the voices of educators have not been adequately included in the conversations leading to the development of standards or in their eventual implementation. And, in the absence of those voices, schools have found themselves at the receiving end of the funnel, with new requirements and expectations pouring into classrooms that are already weighted down with enormous curricular expectations. Decisions made by distant committees, elected officials, and sometimes bureaucrats reflect, at best, limited understanding of the day-to-day realities of adolescents: their needs, their interests, their motivations, and more. It would be easy to point a finger in blame for the shortsightedness of legislative acts such as No Child Left Behind, of policies that establish tests intended to predict first-year college success as high school exit exams, and of imposition of standardized end-of-grade tests on all students regardless of their circumstance.

Certainly, nothing is more difficult to create than good policy and legislation. Though a particular policy or law may appear sound in the first analysis, it is critical, even though time-consuming, that all legislative acts be unpacked to discover the many long-term and far-reaching implications of their implementation. For example, holding teachers and students accountable for using instructional time wisely and for achieving academic gains is entirely reasonable. But what happens when accountability translates to tests that favor some populations over others, focus on information that may not reflect the standards teachers are told to teach, and lead to *real*, and extraordinarily negative, consequences for teachers and schools? These are questions that must be investigated before policies and laws are enacted. And unfortunately, in the most recent wave of reform initiatives—including standards, policy, and legislation—the voices of educators have been lacking and their enormously important perspective has been lost.

None of this has to be the case. But if we, as educators, want a voice at the table, we must be willing to be involved. We must be clear about what we do in the classroom, why we do those things, and what research supports our practice. We must take on the responsibility of trying new things, carefully studying the impact of particular practices, and communicating to others about our work and our findings. And we must be willing to take on advocacy roles as we reach out beyond our own classrooms and schools to help others benefit from our perspective. By becoming more vocal about the lives and stories that constitute the secondary experience, we can help those who construct policy do so with a dose of reality in mind. Unless we share what we know, policymakers will continue to act in isolation.

As leaders in school districts, principals and curriculum directors have great opportunity to support teachers in deepening their professionalism by supporting teacher research, facilitating thoughtful professional development, marshaling necessary resources, and supporting teachers as writers who share their classroom stories with parents, elected officials, and others. Fortunately, there are good models to follow for this work.

The final section of this book describes ways that teachers and curriculum leaders are making a difference in their schools and regions. From gaining confidence in their own practice to creating sustained and thoughtful professional development opportunities for teams of teachers, the work that is going on in classrooms and districts around the country is heartening. This work takes place amid escalating change—in our collective understanding of adolescent literacy for the twenty-first century, in evolving literacy standards, and in the continuously changing expectations that pour into classrooms. Change is difficult. Change efforts that do not fully reflect the needs, perspectives, and realities of teachers and students are likely impossible. In this section, then, I offer teachers and local policymakers tools for immediate use and to build their awareness of their own role in taking charge of interpreting and using standards for the improvement of adolescent literacy.

Engaging Our School Community in Conversations about Standards

This document is intended to support conversations at the school and district levels that result in rigorous and relevant curriculum incorporating these content expectations. The expectations should be addressed recursively and with increasing complexity throughout the high school language arts curriculum. (Excerpt, Michigan High School English Language Arts Content Expectation)

As I've talked about throughout this book, national and state literacy standards can offer a map of our discipline, defining essentials that typically have been agreed upon by teachers and other content experts in the field. Most often, standard documents also provide additional specific definitions in the form of content or performance expectations. Some documents provide great detail, while others present expectations in more general terms. In all cases, these "subcategories" attempt to more fully and specifically define a field of study for a particular grade or academic level. The goal, of course, is that your students will achieve a desired level of competency in these areas from their various literacy experiences by the time they exit the grade or level in question.

Although looking at those standards can be daunting at first, you should remember that these new expectations do not represent a complete departure from what is familiar. They do, however, most often include challenges based on evolving national and state understandings of what students need to know and be able to do to be successful in an ever-changing world. Certainly, literacy standards have come to reflect heightened and evolving expectations as our collective assessment of twenty-first-century literacy has crystallized in new ways.

In our discipline, literacy standards point the way, but to borrow a phrase from Louise Rosenblatt, they are essentially "inkspots on a page" until given life by a teacher ("Acid Test", 62). Without a doubt, the power that standards represent depends largely on the quality of conversations, decision making, and implementation controlled by teachers. As teachers who receive new standards for adolescent literacy, it's vital that we find opportunities for individual and collaborative reflection and discussion with colleagues. Even with these resources, it will take a substantial amount of time to move reflection and discussion into practice. And the more expectations change, the more time and support we will need to fully engage and integrate these standards into daily teaching.

Dr. Kathryn Bell of Spring Arbor University notes, "Teachers cannot teach what they have not experienced." Though the statement seems straightforward, it reveals a critical issue related to standards implementation. With new standards, teachers are routinely being asked to adjust instruction to accommodate new research, new technologies, and new understandings about literacy that they themselves may never have experienced. Though no one would ever expect a pilot to fly a new airplane filled with passengers after simply hearing about changes in the instrument panel, nor a surgeon to perform an operation after simply viewing a video about the procedure needed to do the task successfully, teachers are frequently required to implement new standards and expectations with little more than a quick presentation. Asking for such change with little preparation is unlikely to lead to the results desired.

Quality professional development, then, is a key to successful literacy reform. Starting with grade-level conversations among small groups of teachers and then moving out to school-based and district-based discussions provides educators and community members opportunities to think about how new standards are reflected in current practice as well as how current offerings might need to be strengthened to more fully address the changes required. Looking intently at how current curriculum and practices are working and for whom they are working will likely reveal questions that are challenging to consider. If current curriculum and practice do not lead to successful literacy growth for *all* students, educators must contemplate why that is the case and consider how the situation might be changed.

In the development of the Michigan standards, we posed a series of questions to help guide local conversations. These questions were included in the prefatory materials of the standards document to emphasize their importance.

- How are these content standards and expectations already reflected in our curriculum and instruction?
- Where do we need to strengthen our curriculum and instruction to more fully realize the intent of these standards and expectations?
- What opportunities do these standards and expectations present to develop new and strengthen existing curricula, leading to instructional excellence and college or workplace readiness?
- How do we implement these standards and expectations, taking into account what we know about our students, school, and community?
- How will we assess the effectiveness with which our students and schools are meeting these standards and content expectations?
- How can we use school-based assessments (e.g., student portfolios, school-based writing assessments, teacher or classroom research, district-level assessments) to make data driven about teaching and learning?

Certainly, these questions do not suggest a quick or easy afternoon inservice project. In truth, they could provide the scaffold for intense work over years. The benefits, however, are enormous. Decisions that are anchored in such powerful teacher engagement represent the highest and best collaborative thinking and planning.

By looking first at the strengths that exist in current curricular offerings, teachers are able to share information, increase awareness of the excellent instructional models in their schools, and validate their good work for themselves and their parent groups. They can identify texts, instructional units and practices, and projects that have proven particularly successful with adolescents. The academic day and year in secondary settings provide precious little time for teachers to share what is happening in their classrooms or to collaborate on plans. Providing such opportunities at the onset of an implementation process provides both reassurance and an opportunity to share the wealth that already exists in the school.

Discussions about curricular strengths and successes provide an entry for analysis of the ways current curriculum reflects the expectations posed by new standards. One important aspect of this discussion is the identification of the changes in content and intent of new standards. Though many standards documents focus on specific content requirements, others—and particularly teacher-friendly ones—tug toward a curriculum that offers enhanced relevance, authenticity, and interrelatedness of literacy knowledge and skills. These are more difficult conversations, and teachers may begin to sense a need for common goals and outcomes as they identify inconsistencies within their own programs.

Looking at literacy standards implementation as an opportunity for the development of exciting and new initiatives opens the door to all sorts of interesting possibilities. In school after hours, I have observed teachers working together to develop numerous engaging and innovative initiatives, the kinds of initiatives that work the best when developed in conversation with others, including:

- academic service learning projects
- new units of instruction that connect students to primary research through outreach to individuals and organizations
- added emphasis on nonfiction literary and technical texts for reading and writing that often connect adolescents to particular fields of study or real-world problem solving
- enhanced interaction with a broader range of literature reflecting an ever-increasing canon
- opportunities to explore new and unfamiliar genres for writing
- interdisciplinary studies driven by real, and often student-generated, questions

When teachers become immersed in planning new curricular units, they find themselves energized as they encounter new materials and opportunities for personal growth.

Because new standards will inevitably introduce new challenges and expectations, and because current practice will inevitably not reflect a complete match to teacher beliefs about literacy instruction, a certain level of dissonance can be anticipated. Though dissonance is uncomfortable, the hard work involved in resolving it will serve to strengthen literacy programs for more students. Administrators, curriculum directors, and other literacy leaders hold tremendous power to support teachers in the critical professional development work that will be needed to foster change in literacy instruction. They have the ability to marshal resources, plan sustained and thoughtful professional development, engage content experts to work alongside teachers, arrange for time to think and plan, and advocate for teachers with local school boards and other policymakers. And busy, committed teachers who invest time and energy in this endeavor should be conscious and vocal about the kinds of professional development that have been shown to be successful. There are thousands of wonderful examples of this type of supportive professional work. What follows are examples from the two high schools I talked about in Chapter 4: Mid-State High School and University School District.

Regional Support That Works

As described earlier, teachers at Mid-State High School approached initial standards implementation efforts with trepidation. Fortunately, they had the benefit of long-term and thoughtful professional development offered through collaboration with their regional instructional support center and a local university. In her work with teachers from the Mid-State district, Dr. Kathryn Bell of Spring Arbor University realized that they felt particularly ill-equipped to teach the new content expectations for writing, which included process approaches; strategies for gathering ideas and data; organizing information; producing drafts, editing, and polishing; writing for varying rhetorical purposes and audiences and in varying genres; and language and conventions as reflected in the careful choices made by writers.

Kathryn realized how difficult shifting a paradigm for teaching can be and how much teachers deserve and need support over time to do so. In a project that extended over a two-year period, she and Elaine Weber of the Red Cedar Writing Project set about to give teachers opportunities to experience being writers themselves, to read research and practice being researchers themselves, and to create new units of study that included writing in the ways the new standards expected. In addition, the project introduced teachers to the concept of "backward design" planning (Wiggins and McTighe, 22). Within this framework, teachers began by thinking about results: what did they want students *to know* or *be able to do* as a result of instruction? As they considered the results they were hoping to achieve, they planned within the context of content standards, course or program objectives, specific learning outcomes, and essential questions that the unit was designed to address.

Laura, from Mid-State, was immediately attracted to Kathryn's workshop. Over the course of the two-year, three-phase project, Laura had many opportunities to grow as a writer and researcher. Along with colleagues, she learned a host of strategies as she experimented with new genres, sculpted some pieces of writing through a process of peer and instructor feedback, and shared her final drafts with colleagues. In addition, she took on the task of researching methods for teaching writing in this way and discovered professional texts as well as the *NCTE Beliefs about the Teaching of Writing*. And she learned about supportive ways for planning writing instruction through an integrated approach to instruction.

The model that Kathryn and her colleagues used for their workshop reflects many of the same elements as those found in National Writing Project institutes. Two guiding principles—giving teachers the tools for researching, writing, and planning together as well as operating from a teachers-teaching-teachers foundation—have shaped extraordinary professional learning opportunities for teachers since the mid-1970s and continues as one of the most successful professional development models in the country for supporting lasting instructional change.

As Laura began her planning for a new unit, she used the guide in Figure 6.1 to draw on the research she had completed to shape her planning within the context of the *NCTE Beliefs about the Teaching of Writing*. Having this base for planning allowed Laura to think about the core learning she hoped to promote for her students. The questions that she will eventually raise for them will provide the focus for daily planning and the assessments, both formative and summative, that she will use during the three-week study.

Figure 6.1. Laura's Backward Design: Goals and Learning Outcomes

Step 1: Planning for Desired Results—What do we want students to "get"?

| **Established Goals** *Formal, long-term goals: What content standards, course or program objectives, learning outcomes, and essential questions is this unit designed to address?* | *Note: Academic aims include factual, conceptual, procedural, dispositional, and expert-performance-based outputs*

 NCTE Beliefs about the Teaching of Writing

 1. Everyone has the capacity to write, writing can be taught, and teachers can help students become better writers.
 2. People learn to write by writing.
 3. Writing is a process.
 4. Writing is a tool for thinking.
 5. Writing grows out of many different processes.
 6. Conventions of finished and edited texts are important to readers and, therefore, to writers.
 7. Writing and reading are related.
 8. Writing has a complex relationship to talk.
 9. Literate practices are embedded in complicated social relationships.
 10. Composing occurs in different modalities and technologies.
 11. Assessment of writing involves complex, informed, human judgment.

 Learning Outcomes:

 1. Students will grow in writing confidence.
 2. Students will improve writing fluency.
 3. Students will see writing as essential to their experiences.
 4. Students will recognize the important relationship between reading and writing.
 5. Students will recognize how literature connects people through its beauty, connection to human emotions, and ways of portraying universal messages.

 Essential Question: What do effective writing teachers understand, know, and do?

 1. How do students come to see themselves as writers?
 2. How do students understand their connection to others via avenues of literacy? |

Since her work in the Title II initiative focused so directly on writing instruction, Laura built this unit to enhance student writing abilities through all the language arts. The literature used during the study provides the base for the core understandings (see Figure 6.2) that are foundational to the unit's theme focus. Knowledge and skills targeted for writing instruction are woven around an emphasis on quality reading and writing experiences.

Before moving to the selection of materials and the daily planning, Laura considered how she will assess students' progress through the unit (see Figure 6.3). Finally, after a great deal of thinking and planning, Laura arrived at the moment when she could begin to lay out plans for the unit study (see Figure 6.4). As she did so, the framework she created provided her with confidence that the well-crafted lessons she will teach will align with both the standards she is responsible for and the best practices that she has learned. At the end of her planning or at the conclusion of her unit, she may still choose to go back and back-map her lessons against the template of her state standards in the same way that some writers might choose to outline their completed draft to see if there are any gaps in its development.

Figure 6.2. Laura's Backward Design: Core Understandings

Understandings *What big (core) ideas will students come to understand as a result of this unit?*	**Core Understandings:** 1. How can I discover truth about myself and others? 2. What sacrifices would I make for truth? 3. What criteria do I use to judge my values? 4. How will I stand up for what I value? 5. What can I do to realize my dreams for the future? 6. How do I handle others' points of view? 7. What role does empathy play in how I treat others? 8. What power do I have as an individual to affect change? 9. How do I respond to improper use of power? 10. How do I determine when it is appropriate to take social action? 11. What voice do I use to be heard?
Knowledge and Skills *What will students know and be able to do as a result of this unit?*	*Adapted from the Michigan High School Content Expectations Dispositions and Core Idea questions.* 1. *Students will know skills and strategies to help them on their writing journey.* 2. *Students will take ownership of their own writing processes.* 3. *Students will encounter texts and examples that will challenge their ideas, and they will respond with critical thinking strategies in written and oral form.* 4. *Students will plan, draft, revise, edit, and publish original pieces in multiple genres.* 5. *Students will recognize elements of style and writer's craft in exceptional student and professional pieces and emulate them in their own writing.* 6. *Students will participate as part of a writing community.*

Figure 6.3. Laura's Backward Design: Tasks and Evidence

Step 2: Assessment Evidence—How will we know students "get it"?

Performance Tasks	Core Understandings:
How will students demonstrate the desired understandings through authentic performance tasks? What criteria will be used to judge these performances?	1. Students will compile a writer's notebook which includes fast-writes, skills notes, writing assignments in multiple genres, writing assignments in multiple stages of the writing process, and a skills sheet describing the conventions and skills they are addressing in the work. 2. Students will participate in large- and small-group writing conferencing and sharing, contributing to the work of others and taking on the responsibilities of a community member. 3. Students will help design rubrics that represent the characteristics of good writing.
Other Evidence *What other evidence will students provide (quizzes, homework, journals, etc.)? How will students reflect and self-assess their learning?*	1. Students will provide evidence of their learning through metacognitive journaling (writing about their writing), TILTS, quizzes, peer review, writing process logs, and more. 2. Self-assessment and reflection will be required in regular intervals in written form in relation to students' roles as writers and in relation to their roles as members of a community.

Figure 6.4. Laura's Backward Design: Unit Overview

Step 3: Learning Plan—How will we help students "get it"?

Unit Design	Unit Overview:
What instruction and learning experiences will enable students to achieve the desired results?	This unit has a focus on nonfiction and its many forms. Throughout the unit of study, students will be introduced to a longer piece of literature to read as a whole class, *Night*, by Elie Wiesel, and various subgenres of nonfiction. This three-week unit will come on the heels of a community-building unit that established the routines and expectations of the writers' workshop. Students will participate in short, informal writing invitations and more extensive, outside-of-class writing assignments. The prompts will help students generate pieces of nonfiction writing that emulate the style of accomplished writers. Throughout the unit of study, daily and weekly writing assignments and peer review sessions will trigger craft and skills lessons to improve student writing. They will be offered choice and flexibility to compose their final pieces in the nonfiction genre that best supports their context and content. The unit will culminate with a reading jam and an anthology of the students' writing projects.

In Laura's own professional inquiry, she discovered the classroom of Tracy Rosewarne, which has greatly influenced her own thinking and planning (Sipe and Rosewarne). For this particular unit, Laura chose a nonfiction focus through which she will lead her students into a variety of genres that reveal real stories. The readings included in the unit will be varied, representing different perspectives and time periods. These will provide excellent teachable moments for her to focus on building specific reading skills. Students will engage in reading, writing, discussing, and listening every day and in varied ways, but always with a goal that the work they do will build their skills, allow them to use those skills immediately in meaningful ways, and result in products that are authentic.

Laura's representative unit was completed with much support along the way. The workshop with Kathryn provided a carefully developed scaffold for her evolving thinking and planning. Within the workshop she was surrounded by other teachers who have varied skills and diverse expertise. Some have always been writers; others express fear of writing, though they have been embarrassed and hesitant to admit this fact earlier. Hours set aside each day for reading, writing, and research in a self-selected area of interest led these teachers to sense their own growing "expertise" in an area of the discipline. Quality time spent collaborating and thinking with others developed a camaraderie and community that further supports risk-taking and questioning. Laura and her colleagues took on the behaviors of teacher-researchers, teacher-writers, and teacher-instructional planners. And, because they shared this experience over a great deal of time, it is unlikely that they will shed these new and now comfortable roles when they return to their classrooms.

The professional development opportunities provided to Laura and the other Mid-State teachers closely mirror the workshop that the state standards committee in Michigan envisioned for adolescents. And it aligns closely with research that provided the foundation for the *Adolescent Literacy: An NCTE Policy Research Brief*. Honoring the literacy expertise and questions that students bring with them; supporting exploration of relevant questions; building upon areas of interest and motivation; encouraging authentic work that requires and teaches reading, writing, speaking, and listening; and providing for community building through meaningful collaboration all contribute to lasting change—whether the student is in middle school or a postgraduate school workshop. As Kathryn Bell noted, "It is impossible to teach what you have not experienced." Quality professional development allows for that experience.

Though it is unlikely that Laura or her colleagues will address the ninety-one content expectations included in the Michigan standards in this or any unit, she has clearly designed her unit to teach to each of the fourteen standards that her state requires. Over time, as students benefit from different units designed in this manner, they will experience literacy instruction that stretches them in the manner that standards designers intended.

Local Support That Works

The teachers in University School District have benefited for many years from their proximity to two universities and the professional development resources provided there. Sustained, carefully articulated professional development is readily available through graduate and certificate programs as well as the local affiliate of the National Writing Project. In addition, over many years USD has provided numerous short sessions with nationally recognized speakers in the field of literacy, as well as cosponsored longer institutes. In affiliation with a regional educational center, even more sessions covering a range of topics have been available.

When the USD initially engaged in implementation of new literacy standards, the highly professional teachers of the district resisted mandates that they felt to be not in the best interest of their students. Months passed in frustrated exchanges until, ultimately, teacher leaders, working with a new district-level facilitator, developed a plan for moving their standards-based planning for curriculum and assessment forward. Some of these efforts have been discussed in earlier chapters (see Chapter 4), but pertinent here is the role of professional development in both encouraging and resolving the implementation conflict.

Because the district had invested a great deal of time and resources to develop a remarkably strong cadre of teachers, they were in a unique position to address the demands of new literacy standards. They did not need to look to individuals outside of the district for leadership; they had developed their own leaders who could guide curriculum and assessment projects. Teacher leaders in the district were familiar with current research and practice, and they had been engaged in attending and presenting at inservices, workshops, and institutes at the local, regional, state, and national levels. What they needed from their administrators and curriculum leaders was very different from what was needed in districts that had not had the benefits of long-term resources.

USD teachers needed administrators who would assist them in understanding and setting parameters for the state's requirements associated with the implementation of the new literacy standards and the common assessments approved by the state school board; they needed administrators who would provide essential resources to support the project, including time, summer pay, and other logistical resources. And they needed access to state decision makers, too, because they were accustomed to being on the front lines of statewide curriculum efforts.

What the USD teachers did not need, and would not accept, were top-down mandates that were not consistent with what they knew and believed to be good practice. Once it was clear that the district's administration did, in fact, respect and value the teachers as decision makers, progress was quickly made. Teachers met in grade-level groups, shared their most successful instructional units, and investigated current offerings for consistency and appropriateness at the grade level under consideration. In a few short weeks set aside in the summer, they collaborated on a model that provided a balance between consistency of instructional units and innovation that invited full use of unique teacher expertise. This was possible because they had the freedom to translate the state standards and expectations into logical and meaningful outcomes for their grade level. Ultimately, these outcomes provided the foundation for their common assessments as well.

Though this review makes the process sound easy, that was certainly not the case. Teachers invested enormous effort in planning and shaping their standards-based curriculum. To make the process work, they were called upon to exercise significant skill in negotiation, problem solving, and cooperation. They had to trust one another to advocate for professional decisions that would represent the interests of all students and teachers, and they were required to articulate for one another—and ultimately a community of administrators and parents—not only how the work they proposed provided the rigor called for in the standards but also the comparative assessment data required by the state. Moreover, they needed to describe how their planning might address issues of adolescent motivation and engagement that would be essential if the goal of improving literacy for all students could be achieved.

Certainly the teachers of USD had benefited from many available professional development opportunities in the past, and many had flourished in that environment. Nonetheless, this does not suggest that the district can afford to pull back professional development resources. To the contrary, veteran teachers will require support for sophisticated professional development, such as participation in teacher research or in becoming resources for teacher and/or parent workshops themselves. Many will benefit from continued opportunities to participate and present at conferences at all levels. New teachers will require support in accessing the types of experiences that traditionally have been available to veterans. And all of this requires a district commitment of funding, time, and logistical support.

Suggestions to Share with Your Administrators

What can we learn from these two examples about the kinds of support teachers need to create thorough, thoughtful implementation of standards? First, we know that district-level efforts to support implementation of standards that build twenty-first-century literacy skills for adolescents must include substantial investment in professional development. As can readily be seen in the USD example, those efforts must be diversified. Diversification of program delivery for adolescents has been accepted practice for many years. We must now recognize the differences in needs of educators, too. Moreover, district administrators must carefully consider the attributes of the teachers with whom they work. If the district has been progressive and supportive of professional growth of teachers, administrators must recognize and use the expertise that has developed. Professional teachers will not accept top-down mandates that fail to address what they know to be good practice; they are the leaders who will be most instrumental in implementation of standards and expectations that require sustained work to affect instructional change.

Abundant professional development research suggests the wisdom of implementing a series of steps to support teachers in their adoption and implementation of standards. Teachers who are on the front line of implementation can and should have a voice in what professional development might look like. Among the suggestions you might offer your administrators are these:

1. *Conduct an analysis of strengths.* What are the strengths of the teachers and teacher leaders in the district who will be involved in the implementation of instructional change? Knowing the strengths of the group will make it possible to structure experiences that honor existing knowledge and skills, saving both time and money that can better be invested in moving projects forward. This type of analysis will also identify individuals who can help decide on next steps.

2. *Engage teachers from the beginning in the conversation about instructional changes.* It is likely that no one is more prepared to enter the deliberation about potential changes—what is being required, why it is being required, and how the requirements relate to current offerings—than respected teachers who have already demonstrated leadership in literacy education. This suggests in the strongest way that teachers be recognized as a resource that provides essential expertise from the outset, long before any local decisions have been made. The need for outside expertise may be unnecessary if the district has done the work it should have over time.

3. *With teacher involvement, review the new expectations that are to be implemented, and do not hesitate to speak with the leaders who drafted them.* Do not accept secondhand information. Too often the message that is translated to the district level has already fallen victim to bureaucratized simplification. If mandates are being imposed from outside the district, take the time to investigate them thoroughly and never assume there is only one possibility for addressing them. That is seldom the case.

4. *Engage teacher leaders in analysis of the current program within the frame of new expectations.* Consistently ask, how are we meeting these new expectations already? For which students are we meeting them? If not all, how might we meet or exceed these expectations for all of our students?

5. *Trust teacher planning, particularly when teacher leaders are involved.* Teacher leaders have a history of making things happen. They deserve support, and districts can benefit enormously from the rich base of information they offer.

Teachers cannot do what they have not experienced. If the progressive reforms intended to enhance adolescent literacy have a possibility of being realized, it is imperative that teachers, too, benefit from carefully articulated, sustained professional growth. Though the two cases provided here depict very different sets of professional needs, they point to some essential guidelines for involvement of educators in adolescent literacy initiatives. For these initiatives to succeed, teachers must have available the types of growth experiences they need, and those needs are not one-size-fits-all. Smart school districts will recognize the wisdom in supporting growth for all teachers through diversified opportunities, and then drawing upon the expertise of teachers as perhaps the most important resource the district has for continuous improvement.

Chapter Seven

Claiming a Voice

Donnavan's father charged into my classroom, and the scowl on his face brought an instant jolt of adrenalin to my bloodstream. Wasting no time with pleasantries, he dropped a copy of Catcher in the Rye *on the table in front of me. "Can you tell me why you have my son doing this in class?" he demanded. I took a deep breath, turned to meet his glare with a smile, and said, "I'm glad you asked. . . ."*

That's how I would like to remember the encounter that happened in 1975, but of course that memory wouldn't be exactly accurate. Donnavan's father did charge into my classroom, and he did confront me with ill-concealed anger. Not only was he upset about the book we were reading in class, but he was equally disturbed about the memoir that Donnavan was writing as a result of our classroom engagement with Holden Caulfield. And he had every right to ask questions of me. After all, I was his son's teacher and responsible for shaping Donnavan's literacy instruction for the year. Unfortunately, though I could have talked to Donnavan's father in detail about *what* we were doing in class, as a relatively new teacher I was sorely unprepared to explain *why* we were doing these activities, *why* I had made the choices that I'd made, or even *how* those choices were grounded in the research in my discipline. As a consequence, instead of welcoming him into my classroom with a confident smile, I was left feeling attacked and threatened.

I relate this story to my own preservice students as they prepare for student teaching because I want them to realize that it is not enough for us, as teachers, to know what to do in the classroom; we must also know why we are doing it. We must know the expectations represented by state standards and local curriculum as well as the practices and strategies recommended by contemporary research. We must possess a deep content knowledge as well as a passion for sharing our discipline with adolescents. And just as important, we must have solid instructional reasons why we are selecting the assignments and texts we choose to teach and be able to thoughtfully and carefully articulate what we are doing and why we are doing it—for ourselves, our colleagues, our students, and their parents.

In one of the more moving speeches I have heard Regie Routman deliver, she described how we, as educators, have sat back immobilized as individuals and groups who know adolescents far less than we do make decisions that affect everything we do. I'll never forget her final words: "And WE [emphasis hers] are letting them do it." When it comes to making decisions about adolescent literacy, we do not have to "let them do it." As educators, we are perfectly capable of participating in the decision-making process ourselves. Literacy is everybody's business, but if school-based literacy initiatives are to succeed, teachers are the critical link. Too often teachers have felt like powerless recipients of decisions funneled into the classroom by others. It doesn't have to be that way.

As teachers, we have tremendous power. Not only do we hold primary control and responsibility for literacy instruction in our own classrooms, but we also have the ability to help shape decisions about standards *and* their implementation. However, just as the power we exercise within our classrooms requires that we remain on the cutting edge of our profession, our ability to exercise a voice in decisions that are made beyond our instructional setting requires that we be vigilant in our professional involvement. In both cases, our professionalism will make the difference in whether our voice is credible and persuasive in matters that affect the day-to-day lives of our students as well as our own professional existence. Being professional in this sense requires that we maintain a constant sense of intellectual curiosity about our practice, and that we do the very hard work of continually questioning what we do and why we do it within the framework of our professional beliefs.

Claiming Our Professional Presence in Our Classrooms

Articulating my beliefs and then aligning my practice to match them has proven to be an ongoing and continual challenge for me as a teacher. It is with the help of professional networks that I found my way to clarifying my values, thanks to the guidance of leaders such as Kathy Short, Dan Kirby, James Moffett, and, more recently, my colleagues in Michigan. It took me a great deal of reflection on current research and on my own best sense of what is important for adolescent literacy to crystallize the pedagogical beliefs that provide a foundation for my teaching. While my beliefs have continued to evolve across my career, I have developed confidence in them as a basic foundation that supports my practice—whether in a middle school, high school, or college classroom. It took me a long time to develop the confidence to articulate these beliefs and share them with my students, inviting them into the dialogue. Doing so, however, has provided me with confidence to answer not only their questions about "why are we doing this?" but also my own about "why am I choosing to teach this skill, book, strategy, or lesson to these students at this time?"

My pedagogical beliefs represent a firm commitment to particular practices that I have determined to be critical for adolescent (and adult) literacy development, and they have been formulated based on what I've come to understand based on my own learning (my brain), from my own experiences (my gut), and from my empathetic relationship with my own children and my students (my heart). I share these beliefs with students in my classes as a means to illustrate why particular practices are integral to the work we do together. I explain that to create the type of environment for learning that I value, I'll be working from strongly held beliefs that shape my practice in the classroom. For example, I believe that:

- *Learning is an active and social process of collaborating with others.* Therefore, we will immerse ourselves in writing, reading, and responding to professional works and in reading and responding to works produced by peers. We will also engage in collaborative activities that will include discussing various issues, sharing of personal observations, and planning, synthesizing, and presenting as a group.

- *Learning occurs as we make connections to our own experiences.* Therefore, we'll talk, write, and reflect based on our own experiences and investigate our own questions in relation to the materials we are reading and investigating in class.

- *Choice allows learners to connect to their experiences and feel ownership in their own learning.* Therefore, we will have choices in many things. Though choice isn't always an option, we will have many opportunities to read books we choose, write on topics and in genres we choose, and always we'll have choice in the questions we choose to investigate for papers and for presentations.

- *Learning is reflective as well as active.* Therefore, we'll have many opportunities to reflect on what we are learning and observing through talking, writing, reflecting, and self-evaluating.

- *Learning occurs in a multicultural world with many ways of knowing and demonstrating what we know.* Therefore, we will think together about the many differences we discover in literature, and we will explore multiple ways of demonstrating understanding within our curricular setting.

- *Learning is a process of inquiry.* As learners, we have many questions that deserve time and attention. Because of this, we will identify questions, develop strategies for exploring them, conduct research, and share our findings and new understandings with others.

These beliefs, and others, are critical to everything that I do as a teacher. For example, if I believe that literacy and learning are inquiry processes, my decisions as a teacher must reflect this belief. I must plan for opportunities that allow students to think and talk about books they choose to read; read and share books they care about; read, discuss, and reflect on some books with other readers and try their hands at examining the actions of characters through a variety of perspectives that may not be their own; and raise questions about characters, authors, circumstances, and settings, investigating and sharing their emerging understandings.

If I believe that writing is a process, I will create opportunities for students to engage the world of ideas as they come to understand that every mark on the page represents a decision made by a writer because it best conveys the message for a particular purpose and audience through a selected genre; I will demonstrate strategies that young writers can then use independently when needed in their own writing; and I will allow drafts—sometimes many drafts—of written work that is truly important. If I believe that learning is both personal as well as social, I will plan learning opportunities that allow for personal reflection, quiet reading, writing for individual purposes as well as for talking, discussing, planning, and sharing in pairs and small groups.

Knowing my beliefs directs my practice away from some pedagogical practices, too. I may find myself questioning the use of valuable class time for worksheets, word finds, and projects that eat up hours of instructional time with little gain in reading or writing skills, and eschewing formulaic approaches to writing. Knowing what I believe and being consciously present in my own teaching is as much about turning loose of nonproductive practices as it is about pursuing other more productive ones.

Teachers make decisions thousands of times each day, and being thoroughly and consciously grounded in pedagogical beliefs that are anchored in research and good practice allows us to meet challenges at the door with confidence that can only come when we are really secure with what we are doing and why we are doing it. It also provides us with the opportunity to offer our students solid justifications for the content and pedagogy that frame our instructional work.

The process sounds very straightforward, but in truth, it is as recursive as learning itself. Every time I teach a new course, or a class in a new place, or even a new section of a familiar course, I have to ask myself frequently, "Are my actions matching up to my beliefs?" With every choice I make, I must consider once again, "Why am I asking students to do this?" Teaching is all about *dissonance*, and dissonance is *really* uncomfortable. Taking on the stance of a questioning teacher—of a teacher-researcher—means being a risk taker who is brave enough to face the too frequent lack of congruity between beliefs and practice and being willing to do the hard work of building congruence from the dissonance we experience when we find that beliefs and actions do not align. The process isn't easy and it takes time. But if we want to have a voice in shaping our professional world—the world that affects our students every day—being experts in our own teaching is necessary.

In districts like Mid-State and University School District, groups of teachers have worked together to align beliefs, practices, and standards. They have come to understand that they possess great control over what happens with their students in their English language arts classrooms. Musicians look at a musical score and see the notes on a page that provide a basic definition of what a piece might be. It is through the eye, ear, and skill of the musician that music is created. Professional teachers see standards and curriculum documents in much the same way. It is through their eyes, ears, and skill that rich literacy environments are created in the classroom. If they believe in process, authenticity, socially and personally constructed knowledge, and choice, teachers will approach every juncture with a query as to how those beliefs can be evidenced in expectations and assignments. Moreover, they will have the confidence and expertise needed to demonstrate why particular decisions about practice are being made.

Unfortunately, though, being an expert still isn't enough if we hope to influence educational decisions beyond the school level. To influence policy and practice beyond our own classroom, we must share what we know, and help is available to support that process. Teachers who join local affiliates of the National Writing Project, professional organizations such as the National Council of Teachers of English, and/or teacher research groups have many opportunities for support in refining and sharing the stories that reflect the reality of adolescents in the classrooms they teach. And this sharing is critical. Without reality-based teacher stories, policymakers have only the voices of less-informed lobbyists to draw upon as a basis for decision making.

Working individually, we can reach out to parents and community leaders, bringing them into the classroom by explaining and demonstrating why we must pursue particular policies and practices. Working within networks of dedicated teachers, we are able to reach out in ever-widening circles to decision makers—both elected and appointed—at the local, state, and national levels. In *Teachers*

Organizing for Change, for example, Cathy Fleischer carefully documented strategies for literacy advocacy, describing approaches that teachers at a variety of levels have used to reach out to their communities to make a case for literacy. If we want to have a voice in the standards and policies that funnel to our classrooms, we are called upon to become a part of that advocacy effort, too.

In one of my many conversations with Laura from Mid-State, she lamented the pressures that teachers around her are feeling. "So many teachers are experiencing such distress, they've stopped seeing students as students—instead they see numbers: How many fail the test. What the test score is. How many points must be raised so that they won't be listed as a 'failing' school." Of course she references the state exit exam that confronts her high school students. Laura worries that concerns about the test are narrowing the scope of curriculum in some schools despite the work that teachers have done together to reform their program. She is concerned that more and more teachers are beginning to "go through the motions because teaching just isn't enjoyable anymore." And she states emphatically that she "couldn't be angrier that students are taking the ACT and a thirty-minute writing test—at best a factory model of assessment—that is not a reflection of the standards-based curriculum the district advocates."

Laura has a right to be angry. And she is accepting her obligation to tell her story. The more the public learns about what is really important to support adolescent literacy, the more likely it is that policy can be created that stops the vicious circle Laura and others are experiencing. It is up to teachers everywhere to invite decision makers into our classrooms.

Claiming a Professional Voice

Regardless of what point you find yourself in your professional life, you can claim a voice in the advancement of adolescent literacy efforts. Working with a group of trusted colleagues will provide a network of support that will help you to learn new information, to develop a reflective stance, to clarify beliefs through an exploration of research, and to use your knowledge to advocate for policies you believe important. Here are some suggestions to guide the way:

> 1. *Learn all that you can.* Engage in a professional study group, a graduate program, a teacher research group, or any other professional network that will support your study of current research and practice. Join a professional organization that will assist your exploration and offer you the opportunity to learn from other teachers at a variety of levels. Check out professional websites, blogs, and Web seminars. Read professional books, journals, and policy statements that address the questions you have about teaching. The more you know, the more solid your foundation for decision making will be.

2. *Reflect carefully about your own learning history*. Teachers from your past made an impact on you—sometimes positively and sometimes negatively. Think about the teaching behaviors and strategies they exhibited in both cases. Identify those behaviors and strategies that opened the door to literacy for you, that made you feel capable as an emerging literacy learner. What made the difference? Why? How can you replicate those positive attributes in your own teaching?

3. *Reflect carefully on your teaching*. Focus on one student in your classroom who seems disengaged, who doesn't seem to be successful in the way you might want; spend time trying to understand what is going on and then look for new strategies and approaches that might make a positive difference. Think about the lesson that was successful beyond your expectations. What did you do? What strategies did you draw upon? Consider how you can include these more frequently in your teaching. Then think about the lesson that proved to be shockingly less successful than you had thought. Unpack that one, too. What didn't work? Why? What might have worked better?

4. *Clarify your beliefs about the teaching of literacy*. What is "bottom line" for you? If you had to write down in simple sentences the five or six core beliefs you have that govern all that you do in your English language arts classroom, what would they be? Think carefully about your knowledge of the field and all the reflection that you have done as you craft these statements. Be sure to talk with trusted colleagues throughout this process, and feel free to shape and reshape your list based on your collaborative and emerging understanding.

5. *Align your practice and your beliefs*. Look closely at a unit of study or even a daily lesson plan. Do the choices you have made reflect the beliefs you profess? Have you selected goals or outcomes, strategies, activities, materials, and assessments that reflect what you really believe to be important? Remember, teaching is about dealing with dissonance, about moving from misalignment between beliefs and practice to congruence. It isn't a simple process, but once it is firmly ingrained in your professional thinking, you'll find yourself far more prepared to explain your decisions and to resist mandates that make no sense for your students.

6. *Share your understandings with others*. As you develop strength in your knowledge and practice, open up your classroom. Invite in other teachers, parents, community members, school board members, and elected officials as often as you can. The more good practice they see, the better prepared they are to support your work. The more they know about adolescents, the better prepared they will be to craft policies that help, and not hurt, literacy instruction. Tell your classroom stories at school and district inservices, to community groups, at state and national conferences, in local newspapers, and in professional literature—both electronic and print. Remember, the most popular books for teachers right now are ones written by teachers. Help others see the reality of

what is needed to support *real* literacy growth for *real* adolescents in *real* classrooms.

   7. *Advocate for policies, reforms, standards, and assessments that make sense.* As a teacher, your practice is informed by your head, your gut, and your heart. You know a great deal about adolescents and about literacy. Get involved in networks that will support your efforts to reach out to policymakers and legislators who have direct influence on much that affects your daily work.

Certainly, the vision of teachers as professional, reflective advocates for literacy requires a commitment that goes far beyond the traditional roles educators have held. Yet no one is in a position to know more about the many factors affecting adolescent literacy than teachers. If adolescent literacy initiatives are to be successful, teachers must assume the roles of advocate and leader.

Postscript

Where to from Here?

Over 8 million students in grades 4–12 read below grade level, and 3,000 students with limited literacy skills drop out of high school every school day. (*NCTE Principles of Adolescent Literacy Reform*, April 2006, 2)

For more than three decades, adolescent literacy has been a consistent source of concern. Anchored initially in questions about equity and access, educators have struggled to shape curricula that extend rich literacy experiences to an increasingly diverse student population. Yet as recently as 2006, NCTE reports that more than eight million students in grades 4–12 read below grade level. How many students struggle with writing is subject to much speculation, but certainly there is little reason to assume that there are fewer concerns regarding written communication than about reading. Abundant evidence that documents the relationship between inadequate literacy skills and future academic and workplace struggles underscores the critical nature of this national problem.

It is not the case that the crisis in adolescent literacy has been ignored. To the contrary, during this same period countless outstanding efforts have drawn educators, administrators, and policymakers into collaborative efforts that have created lasting and positive changes in literacy instruction. The National Writing Project, the National Council of Teachers of English, the International Reading Association, and the National Communication Association have sponsored workshops, conferences, and institutes and sustained professional conversations to support teachers who are working to improve literacy instruction in all regions of the country. Other groups, such as the College Board, have designed and sponsored workshops and symposia as well. Advanced Placement workshops offered by the College Board, for example, have targeted instruction for college-bound students and substantially raised the level of challenge in those classes. And many others have been involved as well. The dilemma that continues to this day rests with this question: how do we extend the excellent work that has raised literacy standards for *some* to *all* of our students?

All students deserve to have the ability to fully participate in the society of their future. They require strong literacy skills to do so. To offer less is to guarantee that some will have a more limited voice, more limited opportunities, and more discrimination in almost everything that they do—from seeking and securing jobs to running for public office to enjoying the rich cultural heritages and opportunities our country has to offer. There is no quick or easy fix for addressing the adolescent literacy challenges we face, and, indeed, we should be most wary of anyone who promises a simplistic path to doing so or a reductive method of determining success.

Well-crafted standards hold promise for helping to provide the types of literacy opportunities that we seek, but only if standards are accompanied by curricula and assessment that are consistent with the highest intent inherent in the standards movement and are put into practice by teachers who are knowledgeable professionals. To offer less is to ensure that literacy initiatives will fall short of their promise, and that is a possibility that we simply cannot accept.

Appendix

Mid-State Plan

FIRST TRIMESTER	RESOURCES	MICHIGAN STANDARDS	ACTIVITIES
Six weeks **"HEROES: Be a Hero"**	*Fahrenheit 451* with abridged CDs for levels 1–3	1.1.1, 1.1.3, 1.2.2, 4.1.1	Reflection journal (including drawings/sketches)
		1.1.2	Theme analysis prewriting
			Theme analysis essay answers
		1.1.3, 1.1.4, 1.1.5, 1.1.6, 1.1.7, 1.1.8, 4.1.5	Small-group chapter chunking/ presentations
		1.3.7, 1.3.8, 1.3.6, 1.5.1, 1.5.2, 1.5.3, 1.5.4, 1.5.5	Prereading exploration
		2.1.1, 2.1.2	Recognizing vocabulary in context
		2.1.3	Class discussion (whole group and small group)
		2.1.4, 2.1.5, 2.1.11, 2.1.12, 2.2.2, 4.1.3	Breakdown/exploration of story elements
		2.2.1, 3.1.1	Breakdown/exploration of literary devices
		3.1.2, 3.1.3, 3.1.9	Reading the novel (individually and in class)
		2.3.1, 2.3.2, 2.3.5, 2.3.6, 2.3.7	
	Star Wars—film *Glory*—movie clips *Beyond Rangoon*—media clips	2.1.6, 2.1.8, 2.1.9, 2.1.10	Film excerpts
	"The Sword and the Stone"—short story from text "The Tale of Sir Lancelot"—short story from text "The Hero"—short story by Sue Ragland	3.1.2, 3.1.3, 3.1.9	Explore short story elements
		3.2.1	Discuss short story genre
		2.1.1, 2.1.2, 2.1.11, 2.1.12	Prereading/reading/post-reading
		2.2.2, 2.2.3, 2.3.2, 3.1.1, 3.3.1, 3.3.2	Discussion/journaling
	Warriors Don't Cry—novel excerpts	1.1.1, 1.1.3, 1.2.2, 4.1.1	Reflection journal
		2.1.4, 2.1.5, 2.1.11, 2.1.12, 2.2.2, 4.1.3	Class discussion (whole group and small group)
		2.3.1, 2.3.2, 2.3.5, 2.3.6, 2.3.7	Reading the novel excerpt (individually and in class)
		3.1.7, 3.1.9, 3.1.10	Personal response/narrative writing

"A Wreath for Emmett Till"—Poetry "The Hero"—poem from text "Mother to Son"—poem "Ex-Basketball Player"—poem	3.2.1, 3.2.2, 3.2.4, 3.3.4, 4.2.1, 1.3.1	
Kent State Massacre—news article Operation Homecoming—television news program Rosa Parks—handout *The Murder of Emmett Till*—documentary clips Tiananmen Square—article, pictures, lyrics	1.1.3, 1.2.2, 1.3.6, 1.3.7, 1.3.8, 1.4.4, 2.1.11, 2.1.12 2.1.9, 2.1.10, 2.2.2, 2.2.3 2.3.4, 3.4.1, 3.4.2, 3.4.3, 3.4.4	Written response (formal and informal) Discussion (large and small group) Media focus activity
Persuasive writing—handouts and rubric	1.1.1 — strategies for planning, drafting, revising, editing 1.1.2 — variety of prewriting strategies 1.1.3 — select and use appropriate language 1.1.4 — compose to argue a position/express opinion while paying attention to conventions 1.1.5 — revise to more fully/precisely convey meaning 1.1.6 — edit for sentence variety, fluency, flow 1.1.7 — edit for style, tone, word choice, and conventions appropriate for audience 1.1.8 — proofread for spelling, layout, font 1.3.2 — five-paragraph structure with transitions 1.3.4 — five-paragraph persuasive essay with refutation	
Kite Runner—novel (*A Thousand Splendid Suns*—novel—for students who have read *Kite Runner*) for level 4	2.1.1, 2.1.2, 2.1.5, 2.1.10, 2.1.11, 2.1.12, 2.2.2, 2.2.3, 3.1.5, 3.1.7, 3.1.8 2.1.3, 2.2.1, 2.2.2, 2.2.3, 2.3.2, 2.3.5, 2.3.6 1.3.8, 2.1.11, 2.1.12, 2.3.7, 3.1.7, 4.1.3 3.1.2, 3.1.9 2.2.3, 3.1.2, 3.1.4, 3.1.8, 3.1.9, 3.1.10 2.2.1, 3.1.1, 3.1.2, 3.1.3, 3.1.4, 3.1.9 2.1.3, 4.1.2 1.3.8, 1.3.9, 1.5.1, 1.5.2, 1.5.5, 2.1.10, 2.1.11	Prereading building knowledge of culture Independent reading Book talk/discussion/debate Character analysis Theme analysis Literary elements Vocabulary in context Group presentations Informal writing Formal writing

		1.1.3, 1.2.2, 1.2.3, 2.1.7, 2.3.6, 3.3.5 Standard 1.1, 4.1.5	Compare to an excerpt from *A Thousand Splendid Suns* (feminine protagonist)
			Film excerpts
		3.1.5	
		2.1.6, 2.1.8, 2.1.9, 2.1.10	
	Speak—novel for levels 1–3		Survival guide for ninth graders
	News article on boys who acted in movie forced to flee	3.1.7, 3.1.8, 3.1.9, 3.1.10	

Annotated Bibliography

United States Congress
Goals 2000 or Goals 2000: Educate America Act
Washington, D.C.: U.S. G.P.O., 1994

It's easy to see how *A Nation at Risk* paved the pathway to Goals 2000, or Goals 2000: Educate America Act, passed by the 103rd Congress on January 25, 1994. This document set in motion the national standards movement. Though the document included many different types of goals, eight specifically addressed education. These eight goals included expectations for

- learning readiness for preschool children;
- an increase in high school graduation to at least 90 percent;
- demonstrated competency over challenging subject matter in nine major disciplines; and
- specific achievement targets in science, math, and citizenship.

The document specifically called for the development of *national standards* in targeted disciplines, including English language arts, and it supported the notion of tests to document student achievement in relation to required standards. (www. ed.gov/legislation/GOALS2000/TheAct/index. html)

United States National Commission on Excellence in Education
A Nation at Risk
Washington, D.C.: National Commission on Excellence in Education: [Supt. of Docs., U.S. G.P.O. distributor], 1983

A Nation at Risk recently celebrated its twenty-fifth birthday, encouraging me to ponder the rush of reform efforts—including policies, standards, and legislation—that it initiated. Since I first read *A Nation at Risk*, literally thousands of pages of reports, studies, policies, standards, tests, and acts of legislation have been written—and most trace roots to *A Nation at Risk*. The document was created by the National Commission on Excellence in Education (1983) whose members were charged to examine the quality of education in the United States and to issue a report within eighteen months of its first meeting. Even the short quote included in this book will suggest the alarmist tone of this report that described the country's deteriorating economic position in the world and placed the blame on our educational system. While *A Nation at Risk* did document the high value Americans place on education, it ignored the enormous accomplishments schools, teachers, and students have attained, and it ignored the many complex societal circumstances that affect student success. The report did, however, ignite a firestorm of public and legislative concern. In essence, the report pronounced American schools failures and demanded they be fixed. (www.ed.gov/pubs/NatAtRisk)

National Standards

National Council of Teachers of English/International Reading Association
Standards for the English Language Arts
National Council of Teachers of English, 1111 W. Kenyon Road, Urbana, IL 61801-1096; International Reading Association, 800 Barksdale Road, P.O. Box 8139, Newark, DE 19714-8139, 1996

Many national professional organizations accepted the challenge to develop standards in their disciplines. Among the national standards that were developed, *Standards for the English Language Arts* (1996), published through collaborative efforts of the National Council of Teachers of English and the International Reading Association, was unique in several ways. First, the process of developing these standards was remarkably inclusive, reaching out to teachers from one end of the country to the other; even in Alaska, my colleagues and I were able to provide input and feedback. Second, the authors of these standards chose not to catalog all the many bits of content, strategies, and skills that students could possibly know, but instead provided twelve integrated umbrella standards to help local educators shape programs. Finally, the authors of the *Standards for the English Language Arts* refused to establish expectations for schools, teachers, and students without also addressing issues of access to resources and training for teachers. They also insisted on framing expectations for student and teacher accountability within an understanding of the complex context in which learning takes place. Both NCTE and IRA have worked hard for more than a decade to provide a rich array of books, articles, research reports, policy briefs, and training opportunities (written, face-to-face, and online) to support local teachers and administrators in translating standards into curricula that raise the opportunity level for all students. (www.ncte.org)

National Council of Teachers of English
NCTE Beliefs about the Teaching of Writing
National Council of Teachers of English, 2003

NCTE Beliefs about the Teaching of Writing (2003) is one of the policy documents that has provided help and guidance for teachers and administrators around the country as they have worked toward revising their written communication curriculum. The adolescent literacy policy brief focused upon in this book has been another enormously influential document that has provided assistance in curricular planning. Both are available from the NCTE website. (www.ncte.org)

State Standards

By 1996, when the Goals 2000: Educate America Act was amended, the executive summary reported that sweeping educational reform initiatives already had taken root in forty-seven states and in the District of Columbia and Puerto Rico. By that point thirty-six states already had developed their own standards, too. Of special interest to me was the fact that in both Alaska and Michigan—the

two states in which I was most involved in state-level standards development—groups of teachers had worked countless hours to craft standards that attempted to reflect the complex and interdisciplinary nature of literacy education. Eventually, both states would be called upon to "tighten" those standards in order to raise the level of rigor and challenge for all students in response to federal and other mandates.

As described in this book, the development of state standards is a politically charged and complicated process of compromises. Many voices are reflected in any state standards document, and too often standards and expectations are provided in formats that do not clarify whether one standard is more or less deserving of instructional time than another. Of even greater concern to me is the unfortunate effect of creating documents that appear more like checklists than integrated standards. While detailed listings of expectations provide a definition of standards, an unfortunate consequence is that they may support testing better than they inform instruction.

It is important to note that state standards across the nation share many similarities. For example, most call for literary experiences that span authors, time periods, movements, genres, and more. Standards generally outline expectations for writing that cover a variety of purposes, audiences, and genres. However, state standards also reflect the unique flavor of their locale and the needs of the students who live there. The tension between national efforts to *standardize* the *standards* and state efforts to respond to local needs has led independent groups such as Achieve, Inc., the College Board, and others to provide benchmarks for state standards development.

Others in the Conversation

Achieve, Inc.
Closing the Expectations Gap 2008
Washington, D.C.: Achieve, Inc., 2008

This is the latest edition of Achieve's annual report on the progress of each of the fifty states toward aligning their state standards with college expectations as described in *Ready or Not*. As noted earlier, the standards created by Achieve have not been endorsed by the major professional organizations most intimately involved with literacy education. As a consequence, I remain concerned about efforts to require states to alter their own standards in order to align with those of Achieve.

American Diploma Project
Ready or Not: Creating a High School Diploma That Counts
Washington, D.C.: Achieve, Inc., 2004

This book documents concerns of an independent, bipartisan group, Achieve, Inc., that the high school diploma has lost its value and validity because schools have not held themselves and their students to sufficiently high standards for academic achievement. To remedy this situation, Achieve has created a set of standards for English language arts that reflects traditional expectations for literature and composition studies. In *Ready or Not*, these authors also describe expectations for schools to develop measures of accountability that document and track student progress. While many groups have also developed standards that weigh in on state efforts, Achieve has gained enormous power to review and require alignment of state standards with their independently developed ones. I remain alarmed that the Achieve standards for English have not been vetted by either NCTE or IRA and likely do not fully reflect the beliefs of either organization. (www.achieve.org)

Friedman, Tom
The World Is Flat
New York: Farrar, Straus, and Giroux, 2005

This book should be read and discussed by educators everywhere. In this highly informative book, Friedman provides detailed discussion of what our students face as they move from school to the marketplace. With great detail, he demonstrates how the technologically connected world of the twenty-first century will demand academic prowess of our students as they compete for jobs on a global stage.

Works Cited

Achieve, Inc. *Closing the Expectations Gap 2008: An Annual 50-State Progress Report on the Alignment of High School Policies with the Demands of College and Careers*. Washington: Achieve, 2008. Print.

———. *Ready or Not: Creating a High School Diploma That Counts*. Washington: Achieve, 2004. Web. 23 Feb. 2009.

———. *Rising to the Challenge: Are High School Graduates Prepared for College and Work, A Study of Recent High School Graduates, College Instructors, and Employers*. Washington: Achieve, Feb. 2005. Web. 23 Feb. 2009. Appleman, Deborah. *Critical Encounters in High School English: Teaching Literary Theory to Adolescents*. New York: Teachers College; Urbana: NCTE, 2000. Print.

Atwell, Nancie. *In the Middle: New Understandings about Writing, Reading, and Learning*. 2nd ed. Portsmouth: Boynton, 1998. Print.

Berliner, David C., and Bruce C. Biddle. *The Manufactured Crisis: Myths, Fraud, and the Attack on America's Public Schools*. Cambridge: Perseus, 1995. Print.

Bloom, Benjamin S., ed. *Taxonomy of Educational Objectives: The Classification of Educational Goals*. New York: Longman, 1984. Print.

College Board. *Standards for College Success*. New York: College Board, 2004. Print.

Conley, David T. *Understanding University Success: A Report from Standards for Success*. Eugene: Center for Educational Policy Research, 2003. Print.

"Creating a 21st Century Michigan Workforce: A State Roundtable." Lt. Governor's Commission on Higher Education and Economic Growth, Dec. 2004. Web. 20 Feb. 2009.

Fiske, Edward B. "A Nation at a Loss." *New York Times* 25 Apr. 2008. Print.

Fleischer, Cathy. *Teachers Organizing for Change: Making Literacy Learning Everybody's Business*. Urbana: NCTE, 2000. Print.

Friedman, Thomas L. *The World Is Flat: A Brief History of the Twenty-First Century*. New York, Farrar, 2006. Print.

Goals 2000: Educate America Act. Pub. L. 103–227. 25 Jan. 1994. Web. 20 Feb. 2009.

Graves, Donald H. *A Researcher Learns to Write: Selected Articles and Monographs*. Exeter: Heinemann, 1984. Print.

Michigan Dept. of Education. *High School Content Expectations: English Language Arts*. Lansing: Michigan Dept. of Education, Apr. 2006. Print.

Myers, Miles. *Changing Our Minds: Negotiating English and Literacy*. Urbana: NCTE, 1996. Print.

National Commission on Excellence in Education. *A Nation at Risk: The Imperative for Educational Reform*. Washington: GPO, 1983. Print.

National Council of Teachers of English. *NCTE Beliefs about the Teaching of Writing*. Urbana: NCTE, Nov. 2004. Web.

National Council of Teachers of English. *NCTE Principles of Adolescent Literacy Reform: A Policy Research Brief*. Urbana: NCTE, Apr. 2006. Print.

National Council of Teachers of English, and International Reading Association. *Standards for the English Language Arts*. Urbana: NCTE; Newark: IRA, 1996. Print.

Nehring, James H. "Conspiracy Theory: Lessons for Leaders from Two Centuries of School Reform." *Phi Delta Kappan* 88.6 (2007): 425–32. Print.

Romano, Tom. *Blending Genre, Altering Style: Writing Multigenre Papers*. Portsmouth: Boynton, 2000. Print.

Rosenblatt, Louise M. "The Acid Test for Literature Teaching." *Making Meaning with Texts: Selected Essays*. Portsmouth: Heinemann, 2005. 62–71. Print. Rpt. from *English Journal* 45.2 (1956): 66–74.

———. *The Reader, the Text, the Poem: The Transactional Theory of the Literary Work*. Carbondale: Southern Illinois UP, 1978. Print.

Sipe, Rebecca Bowers, and Tracy Rosewarne. *Purposeful Writing: Genre Study in the Secondary Writing Workshop*. Portsmouth: Heinemann, 2006. Print.

Smith, Michael W., and Jeffrey Wilhelm. *"Reading Don't Fix No Chevys": Literacy in the Lives of Young Men*. Portsmouth: Heinemann, 2002. Print.

Stedman, Lawrence C., and Carl F. Kaestle. "Literacy and Reading Performance in the United States, from 1800 to the Present." *Reading Research Quarterly* 22.1 (1987): 8–46. Print.

United States Dept. of Labor. The Secretary's Commission on Achieving Necessary Skills. *What Work Requires of Schools: A SCANS Report for America 2000*. Washington: GPO, 1991. Print.

Wiggins, Grant P., and Jay McTighe. *Understanding by Design*. Alexandra, Va.: Association for Supervision and Curriculum Development, 1998.

Index

Author

A former secondary English teacher and K–12 curriculum coordinator for English/language arts in the remarkably diverse Anchorage School District in Alaska, Rebecca Bowers Sipe now serves as the head of the Department of English Language and Literature and professor of English education at Eastern Michigan University. She was a participant in the first National Writing Project Invitational Institute in Alaska and later served as the project's site coordinator. Upon moving to Michigan, she immediately affiliated with the Eastern Michigan Writing Project, where she continues her collaboration with site directors and teacher leaders on various research projects.

Sipe has been involved in investigating ways to improve literacy instruction for all students for three decades, an interest that has led to extensive involvement in curriculum and standards development in multiple states and on a variety of national projects. She is a past chair of the NCTE Secondary Section Steering Committee and chaired the study group that developed the *NCTE Beliefs about the Teaching of Writing*. Her interest in supporting students who struggle with literacy continues to be a driving force in her research and writing. Publications include a genre-based composition series for elementary students, *Strategies for Writing*; two professional books written in collaboration with Eastern Michigan Writing Project teacher leaders, including *They Still Can't Spell? Understanding and Supporting Challenged Spellers in Middle and High School* (with Dawn Putnam, Karen Reed-Nordwall, Tracy Rosewarne, and Jennifer Walsh) and *Purposeful Writing: Genre Study in the Secondary Writing Workshop* (with Tracy Rosewarne); and articles and book chapters. Sipe also presents frequently on a variety of teaching and policy issues.

This book was typeset in Jansen Text and BotonBQ by
Barbara Frazier.

Typefaces used on the cover include American Typewriter,
Frutiger Bold, Formata Light, and Formata Bold.

The book was printed on 60-lb Williamsburg Recycled Offset
paper by Versa Press, Inc.

30% Total Recycled Fiber